Praise for *Coop*

"*Cooperative and Connected* is
with children must read it!"
—Violet Oaklander, Ph.D., Gestalt therapist,
author of *Windows to Our Children*

"In her book, *Cooperative and Connected*, Dr. Solter integrates a really nuts-and-bolts guide to practical parenting questions with vignettes that perfectly illustrate her points. And overarching all of this is her compassionate, kind, nurturing approach to parenting. I will definitely recommend it to parents."
—Thomas Armstrong, Ph.D., author of
The Myth of the ADHD Child

"In her book, *Cooperative and Connected*, Aletha Solter has given parents a magnificent guide to help develop a truly cooperative relationship with their children. Her approach avoids the conflicts that result in the oppositional behaviors of the 'terrible twos' and fosters self-assured, compassionate children. With all the theories and rules about child development, her book stands out, providing a deceptively simple set of principles that will ensure the greatest gift you can give to your kids, and even to our future society."
—Peter A. Levine, Ph.D., author of
Trauma-Proofing Your Kids

"I read *Cooperative and Connected* with fascination because of the gentleness of Dr. Solter's approach and her creative suggestions for how to stay gentle and feel competent, even when a child is screaming or refusing to obey. This seems like a revolutionary book, a MUST read for all parents, but especially for parents of highly sensitive children."
—Elaine Aron, Ph.D., author of *The Highly Sensitive Child*

Cooperative and Connected

Cooperative and Connected

Helping Children Flourish
without Punishments or Rewards

Aletha J. Solter, PH.D.

SHINING STAR PRESS ★ GOLETA, CALIFORNIA

A previous edition of this book was published in 1989 with the title *Helping Young Children Flourish*.

Published by Shining Star Press
Post Office Box 206
Goleta, California 93116, U.S.A.
Phone & Fax: (805) 968-1868
Email: info@awareparenting.com
Website: www.awareparenting.com (The Aware Parenting Institute)

Book design: Studio E Books, Santa Barbara

Cover photo credit: iStock.com/BraunS

Second printing 2019

PUBLISHER'S CATALOGING INFORMATION
Solter, Aletha Jauch, 1945–
Cooperative and connected: helping children flourish without punishments or rewards / Aletha J. Solter
Continues: The aware baby.
Includes bibliographical references.
ISBN: 978-0-9613073-9-4
1. Child psychology. 2. Child rearing. 3. Parenting. 4. Parent and child. I. Title.
Dewey Decimal Classification: 649.1
Library of Congress Control Number: 2017919311

"If we are to attain real peace in this world, we will have to begin with the children."

—Gandhi

Acknowledgments

I would like to express my gratitude to my friends and colleagues who suggested that I write the first edition of this book (in 1989). I am also grateful to all the parents who let me interview them. Their names and those of their children have been changed (except for those of my own children, used with their permission). I have kept many of these examples in this revised edition. I would also like to acknowledge my clients and workshop attendees around the world who have given me new insights and helped me clarify this approach by asking questions and sharing their experiences. Finally, I would like to thank the people who gave me feedback for this new edition. The following people read all or parts of the manuscript and made helpful suggestions: my husband, Ken Solter, my son, Nicholas Solter, my daughter-in-law, Sonja Solter, my daughter, Sarah Solter, and my colleague, Heather Stevenson.

Contents

List of Charts

Warning/Disclaimer

This book is an educational resource for parents focusing on the developmental, emotional, and educational needs of children between two and eight years of age. It is not intended to be a substitute for medical, psychological, or educational advice or treatment. Some of the behaviors and symptoms mentioned in this book can be an indication of serious emotional, medical, behavioral, or developmental disorders. If your child is suffering from problems of any kind, you are strongly advised to seek professional advice and treatment from competent professionals. Some of the suggestions in this book may not be appropriate under all conditions or with all children. The author and publisher offer no guarantee for the effectiveness of the suggestions in this book, and they shall have neither liability nor responsibility to any person or entity with respect to any damage caused, or alleged to be caused, directly or indirectly by the information contained in this book.

Preface to the New Edition

This book was first published in 1989 with the title, *Helping Young Children Flourish*. It is a sequel to *The Aware Baby*, and these first two books describe the complete Aware Parenting approach from birth to age eight. I have written three other books that focus on specific aspects of this approach: *Tears and Tantrums*, *Attachment Play*, and *Raising Drug-Free Kids*. I am delighted that my books have been translated into many languages.

For this revised and updated edition (with a new title), I have kept the basic organization, but I have included new information, insights, and summary charts. Research studies continue to validate and support this approach to parenting, and I am pleased to share some of these more recent research findings in this new edition.

This book contains many examples of my own children, who are now adults. I can say with confidence that this approach works. I never used punishments or rewards, and my children never rebelled, because they didn't have anything to rebel against. My husband and I enjoy a close relationship with both of them. I am thrilled that our grandchildren are being raised with this approach, and they, too, are flourishing.

In 1990, I founded the Aware Parenting Institute to help spread this approach around the world. I developed a certification program for people who want to teach this approach to parents, and there are now certified instructors in many countries. Please see the Aware Parenting website for more information: www.awareparenting.com.

Cooperative and Connected

Introduction

THIS BOOK COVERS the period from two to eight years, normally referred to as early childhood. It is a sequel to *The Aware Baby* (birth to age two-and-a-half). You do not need to read *The Aware Baby* in order to understand the present book, which is self-explanatory and complete in itself. However, if you wish to gain a deeper understanding of babies' emotional needs and development, *The Aware Baby* may provide you with some insights and helpful information.

The approach described in this book is based on research in the fields of attachment, trauma, child development, neurophysiology, and psychotherapy. It focuses on children's emotional and developmental needs and on the parent/child relationship. Thanks to research psychologists, there is a wealth of information about young children's development, and we now have a fairly clear idea of how they learn and which factors can enhance or hamper their development. An important finding is that our brains are shaped by experience. The way we treat young children will determine how their brains function later on. Early experiences (beginning in the womb) can even determine which genes will be expressed and which will remain dormant. The implication of these research findings is that parents matter.

Traditional behavioral approaches, which use rewards or punishments, can produce obedient children who will passively accept the status quo. This approach may be appropriate for training factory workers. However, it will not enhance children's ability to find solutions for problems that they have not encountered before. We need innovative thinkers to solve all the problems that are relatively new for human beings: How to cope with ten thousand families whose homes have been flooded? What to do with the plastic waste in the oceans? How to harness new forms of energy? How to prevent young people from joining terrorist groups? How to avoid widespread addiction to narcotic drugs? What can we do to end poverty?

We need a new approach for raising children. Our challenge as parents is to create a new generation of compassionate and competent people who will have the motivation, courage, creativity, and skills to find solutions for the problems facing humanity. It is time to question traditional ways of raising children and do something different. This book will help you understand your children, connect with them, and solve behavior problems without the use of either punishments or rewards. With your support, your children can develop their full potential for thinking, learning, coping with stress, problem solving, and relating lovingly to others. This approach will help them flourish, lead meaningful lives, and find ways to make the world a better place.

Parenting requires a tremendous amount of time, energy, attention, financial resources, and commitment. You may be struggling with economic hardship, isolation, and emotional or health problems. Perhaps you are a single parent with a full-time job and no free time. One way to make the job of parenting easier is to find help from others. You do not need to raise your children in isolation. If you cannot afford to pay someone, perhaps you can trade help with other parents. If you are tired or sick, ask a friend or neighbor to come over. Do not wait until you are totally exhausted. You owe it to yourself and your children to take good care of yourself and ask for the help you deserve.

As you travel through the early childhood years with your children, you will experience many emotions, both pleasant and painful. You will probably be reminded of incidents from your own childhood, and you may discover that a problem with your child resembles a difficulty you experienced at the same age. In fact, you will probably re-experience your entire childhood, whether you want to or not! If you suffered from unaware parenting or abuse, your child's behavior will trigger your anger, perhaps more frequently than you expected. It is perfectly normal to feel irritated, impatient, angry, frightened, or totally baffled by your child's behavior. But these feelings will need an outlet so they do not interfere with your clear thinking and cause you to act in ways that you may later regret.

One of the most helpful things you can do for yourself (and your children) is to find someone who can listen to you and accept your feelings without judgment or advice. Take time to talk about all your daily upsets: the mud on the rug, night awakenings, sibling fights, bedtime struggles, and tantrums in the supermarket. You will also benefit by sharing your deeper feelings, doubts, and questions: Am I a good parent? Is my child normal? How can I meet my own needs? Will my child succeed in school? What can I do about my anger?

You will probably notice that your stress level decreases after you share your feelings with a supportive listener, and you may find it easier to become the kind of parent you want to be. Some parents benefit by exchanging listening time with their partner or a friend. However, if you are struggling with disturbing feelings of incompetence, depression, anxiety, powerlessness, or rage, you may benefit from professional therapy.

A set of exercises follows each of the chapters in this book. These consist of three sets of personal questions. The first set will help you explore your own childhood, the second encourages you to express your feelings about your child, and the third offers suggestions for ways to nurture yourself. You may choose to work through these exercises by thinking silently or writing in a journal. Another possibility is to answer the questions verbally with a supportive listener.

Don't forget to appreciate yourself for all the wonderful things you do for your children and all the love and attention you give them, even though you may feel inadequate at times. You are probably doing much more than you think!

Chapter 1

Tears and Tantrums

THIS CHAPTER FOCUSES on the reasons for crying and the most helpful way to respond to children's tears and tantrums. Many books for parents consider crying and temper tantrums to be behavior problems that should be discouraged. This chapter offers a different perspective and describes the benefits of crying. I have covered this topic first because this information is important for understanding the rest of the book.

Why do children continue to cry after they have learned how to talk?

You may wonder why your child continues to burst into tears at times, even when she is old enough to express her feelings and needs with words. When she was a baby, you accepted her crying because she didn't know how to talk. You knew that crying was a major form of communication, and you responded in an effort to meet her needs.

Crying is indeed a baby's way of communicating, and that is *one* of the reasons why babies cry. But there is a second, less recognized, reason for crying. It is common for babies to cry even after all of their immediate needs have been filled. Perhaps your baby had crying spells in the late afternoon or early evening, and you couldn't figure out what she needed or how to comfort her. This kind of crying, sometimes called "colic," often worries parents because nothing they do seems effective. There appears to be no way to make the baby happy.

Crying without any obvious cause typically peaks at about six weeks after birth, and this crying is now considered a normal stage of development. It does not necessarily imply that the baby is suffering from physical pain. In fact, much of this crying may even be a beneficial tension release mechanism.

Research studies have found correlations between early stress and crying. The more stress babies experience, the more they cry. For example, babies who had a difficult birth cry more than babies whose births were less complicated. Babies who continue to cry while being held (and after all immediate needs have been met), may be healing from past distressing experiences such as birth trauma. Overstimulation is another source of stress that can cause a need to cry. It's hard to believe that babies have stressful lives, but babies are extremely vulnerable, and they can be easily overwhelmed or even traumatized, even with the best of parenting. For stressed babies, crying functions as a natural stress-release mechanism. (See my book, *The Aware Baby* for a detailed description of stress-release crying during infancy.)

The communication function of crying is gradually replaced by language. Toddlers learn to ask for food when they are hungry, and they learn to say "too cold" when the bath water is too cold. However, stress-release crying is *not* replaced by talking. Children continue to cry in order to recover from sad, frightening, disappointing, frustrating, or overwhelming experiences. Even though older children may verbalize their feelings (for example, "I'm sad that Daddy didn't come home in time for my birthday party"), they may still need to cry in order to recover fully from distressing experiences.

The meaning and purpose of crying have been greatly misunderstood. Many parenting books include crying and tantrums in chapters about discipline, along with other behaviors such as hitting, biting, swearing, lying, and stealing. This negative view of crying is unfortunate, because crying and raging are actually beneficial stress-release mechanisms, which allow children to maintain or restore emotional health. In fact, crying and tantrums may actually help *prevent* the "misbehaviors" with which they are so often listed.

Many parents discover that their children become more cooperative and less aggressive after a good cry.

Another mistaken notion equates crying with hurting, and you may assume that your child will feel better if she would only stop crying. You may therefore think that you will do your child a favor by helping her to stop crying. In reality, however, crying is the process of becoming *unhurt and unstressed.* Children will continue to feel upset and stressed if their crying is cut short. Our role as parents is not to stop our children from crying, but to love and support them so they can fully release their painful emotions.

Is there research evidence that crying is beneficial?

Researchers first became interested in crying back in the 1970's. These early studies found reduced tension after psychotherapy sessions in which clients cried, compared to a control group of people who exercised for an equivalent period of time. The indications of tension reduction included lower blood pressure, pulse rate, and body temperature, as well as more synchronized brain-wave patterns.

In the 1980's, a biochemist named William Frey researched the chemical content of human tears and found differences between emotional tears (during real crying) and those caused by an irritant such as a cut onion. The emotional tears had higher concentrations of substances related to our physiological stress response (such as ACTH and catecholamines). He suggested that the purpose of emotional tears is to remove these substances from the body, just as we remove waste products by urinating and defecating. If these substances were not eliminated, they would maintain the body in a state of tension and hyperarousal. If that condition became chronic, it could lead to stress-related illnesses. Frey suggested that we may increase our susceptibility to a variety of physical and psychological problems when we suppress our tears.

Researchers have found evidence for psychological as well as physical benefits of crying. It counteracts the stress response through activation of the parasympathetic nervous system, and it is recognized as an effective mood enhancer. Studies have shown that crying may help reduce symptoms of asthma, arthritis, and allergic reactions, and also promote recovery and healing in general. These findings point to the conclusion that crying is a beneficial physiological process, which allows people to cope with stress. It's a natural repair mechanism that we are born with, and people of all ages can benefit from a good cry.

What do children need to cry about?

Most parents find it easier to accept their child's crying if they can understand the reasons for it. Unfortunately, young children rarely verbalize their reasons for crying, so you may have no recourse but to guess. Children experience various kinds of stress, and these can all increase their need to cry. Categories of stress include hurts by commission, hurts by omission, and situational hurts. In addition, unhealed trauma from infancy can further contribute to symptoms of stress during the childhood years. I describe each of these sources of stress in the following paragraphs.

The hurts by commission include all the ways that we hurt children, often without realizing it. This category includes physical, sexual, and verbal abuse, teasing, shaming, humiliation, and criticism. It also includes all forms of punishment, as well as racist and sexist stereotypes and other forms of oppression. Additional stress can arise when we force children to do things against their will or when we overschedule their lives. Traditional approaches to education and school discipline can also cause stress. In addition, this category includes hurtful behaviors by other children, such as teasing, bullying, and hitting. Finally, we sometimes unknowingly add an additional layer of stress whenever we discourage children's natural expressions of anger, fear, or sadness.

No parent is perfect. We all have our moments of impatience and unawareness, especially if our own needs are not being met or if we are suffering from the effects of our own painful childhood. Young children are often messy, active, impatient, demanding, curious, fearful, and loud. These behaviors are all natural, and it's important to let children be themselves, even though this acceptance may require a tremendous amount of patience. This doesn't imply that we must always let children do whatever they want. We can strive to set loving limits while remaining calm, because if we react with impatience or anger, our children will feel hurt. It's important to remember that children are very vulnerable and totally dependent on our love and acceptance.

The second category, hurts by omission, refers to unfilled needs. The major needs during early childhood are for food, love, shelter, physical closeness (holding and cuddling), attention, appropriate stimulation, autonomy, respect, and play. Children also need to feel safe, both physically and emotionally. Behavior problems can arise when we fail to meet children's needs, especially those for attention and connection. Children need a great deal of individual attention from adults who are sincerely interested in them and who are willing to listen, play, and answer their questions. Each child needs time every day with someone who thinks he is important and special. Children who must care for themselves after school for several hours a day may be under stress even though they seem to be coping well. Young children need an older person available at all times who assumes caretaking responsibilities and provides companionship and emotional support.

The third category, situational hurts, refers to distressing events caused indirectly by life circumstances. This category includes illnesses and injuries, separation from a parent (because of illness, death, or departure), parental divorce, poverty, natural disasters (fires, floods, earthquakes), and terrorism or war. Stress can also occur during major changes such as the birth of a sibling, a move to a new home, or a new school. Your own stress can affect your children. When you are feeling anxious, overwhelmed, or depressed, they may also feel stressed because of your state of mind. This category also includes developmental fears and frustrations resulting from children's lack of information or skills, as well as overstimulation (more likely for highly sensitive children). Finally, because of an incomplete understanding of cause and effect and the limits of their own power, young children can develop guilt feelings for events that are totally unrelated to their own actions, such as a mother's miscarriage.

In addition to these various sources of stress during the early childhood years, many children have accumulated painful feelings resulting from unhealed stress or trauma during infancy. Our bodies store the memory of our earliest experiences, especially traumatic ones, even though we may not be able to put those memories into words. If your child had a difficult birth, early medical interventions, or a traumatic separation from you, he may have behavior problems later on, which are unrelated to any current source of stress. Babies can heal from these early traumas soon after they occur, but if you didn't have information about how to help your child heal when he was an infant, you can help him now. It's never too late to help your child heal from past trauma.

Sources of stress for young children

• Hurts by commission
  Ex: abuse, punishment, criticism, humiliation, bullying

• Hurts by omission (unmet needs)
  Ex: lack of love, attention, stimulation, autonomy, respect, or time for play

• Situational hurts
  Ex: illness, injury, parental divorce, birth of a sibling, new school

• Unhealed trauma from infancy
  Ex: birth trauma, medical intervention, separation from parents

---

What should I do when my child cries?

You can help and support your distressed child even when you don't know why she is crying. The first step is to remove any obvious source of pain or fright and to fill immediate needs. If another child is hitting her, take steps to stop the aggressive behavior. If she is screaming at the sight of a dog, calmly move her away from the animal. If she hasn't had a turn on the slide, let her have a turn if time permits. After you have done everything possible to make your child feel safe and meet her needs, she may continue to cry. If she does, the most helpful response is to accept the crying without trying to stop it.

It's possible that you were not allowed to cry enough as a child. Your well-meaning, but misinformed, parents may have distracted, punished, or ignored you when you cried. Perhaps you were stopped kindly ("there, there, don't cry") or with a threat ("if you don't stop crying, I'll *give* you something to cry about"). Maybe your parents offered you food, thinking that you were hungry ("have a cookie, it will make you feel better"). If your first impulse is to eat something when you feel anxious or depressed, this craving could be caused by the fact that your parents often fed you when you cried. Perhaps you were sent to your room when you cried or praised for being "good" when you did not cry.

In many cultures, parents tend to be more accepting of their daughters' tears than those of their sons. You may have heard your parents say "big boys don't cry." Many boys learn very early in life to "act like a man" and stop expressing feelings of pain, fear, or sadness. Unfortunately, children tend to enforce these gender stereotypes with each other by teasing boys who cry easily. Researchers have found that, as early as age four, boys tend to cry slightly less than girls during a venipuncture procedure, even though the boys' heart rate increases just as much as that of girls.

When parents use distractions, disapproval, or punishment to stop children from crying, the children learn that their painful emotions are not acceptable, and they begin to repress them in order to please their parents. Unfortunately, when children repeatedly hold back their tears, they eventually lose touch with their feelings. The result of these early experiences is that the children may have great difficulty expressing emotions as adults.

If you were stopped from crying as a child, you may feel uncomfortable around crying children and will want to stop them, just as you yourself were stopped. This reaction is normal. It's not easy to accept our children's tears. With practice, however, it is possible to give your child the right to express her emotions, even though you were denied this freedom as a child.

Some parents wonder what to say when their children cry. The following chart offers some suggestions of helpful ways to respond to a crying child, instead of the typical responses you may have heard as a child. Sometimes you don't need to say anything at all. You can simply pay attention to your child while silently showing love and empathy.

Suggestions of what to say to a crying child

• I hear you. I'm listening.

• It's okay to cry.

• I see how upset you are.

• Do you want a hug?

• I'm right here. You're safe with me.

• I will stay with you until you feel better.

• I won't leave you alone with those big feelings.

• You can cry as long as you want.

• You don't have to explain anything.

• I love you no matter how sad (mad) you are.

It is important to hold babies whenever they cry, but toddlers and older children don't always need to be held. You can offer to hold your child, but let her decide if she wants to come into your arms. Your child may want to snuggle close while sobbing, but at other times, she may prefer more space and freedom for vigorous physical movements while crying.

The following example of my daughter illustrates how I responded to her crying after a small disappointment.

> When Sarah was three years old, I bought a bathing suit for her at a garage sale, and I told her we would go swimming when the weather got warmer, perhaps in a few months. Later on that day the sun came out from behind some clouds. Sarah immediately started to talk about going swimming, thinking that we would be going that very minute because of the sunny weather. She wanted to put on her new bathing suit. I explained to her that we were not going swimming because it was still winter and we would get too cold. She looked very disappointed and burst into tears. I gathered her in my arms and said, "You really wanted to go swimming, didn't you?" She sobbed heavily for a few minutes, and I held her until the crying stopped. Then she became as cheerful as she had been before.

My daughter's disappointment occurred because of her limited concept of time. There was nothing I could do to fix the situation or make her feel better. Once I realized this, there was no point in distracting her away from her feelings, because she needed to express and release them. Young children's lives are full of little upsets, and each one needs to be cried about.

If your child cries because of something hurtful you did, you can apologize while accepting her anger and tears. A father I interviewed described the following situation with his son.

> Today a friend called up, and I hadn't talked to him for a long time, so we got into a great discussion. But right

before my friend called, I had promised to take Kevin (age six) to a friend's house, so he was waiting for me to get off the phone. I kept telling him, "Okay, okay, just a minute." And I really meant just a minute, but it was so much fun talking to my friend that I kept on talking. When I finally hung up the phone, I went outside, and there was Kevin kicking the ground and crying. He said, "You lied." So I held him while he cried, and he said, "But you told me we were going right away, and we didn't, and I waited and waited, and you still didn't get off the phone." Once I understood his point of view, I realized that it was my fault, and I said, "I'm sorry, Kevin. I shouldn't have talked so long." With this approach, I find that I get a lot more cooperation and respect back from him.

You will not always know why your child is crying, and these outbursts with unknown causes may be the most difficult ones to tolerate. However, your child will benefit each time you can find the patience to accept her tears. Try to remember that there is always a valid reason for her crying, even though you might not know what it is.

What about temper tantrums?

Temper tantrums during early childhood are common and normal. Sometimes called "meltdowns," these are episodes of loud, angry crying and screaming accompanied by active body movements. A genuine tantrum is a healthy release of emotional pain and anger resulting from hurtful or frustrating experiences. It's important to distinguish genuine tantrums from aggressive behavior. During a genuine tantrum, there is no aggression or destructiveness. The child makes no attempt to hurt anybody or anything.

When children attempt to harm others or the environment, they are not releasing emotions in a healthy way, probably because they do not feel safe enough to have a genuine tantrum. Perhaps they have been distracted or punished for crying in the past, so they resort to distorted and hurtful expressions of anger. You will need to intervene if your child is hurting others or being destructive. But there is no need to stop a genuine, nonviolent tantrum. The following table compares these two very different ways of expressing anger. (See Chapter 5 for suggestions of ways to deal with aggression and destructiveness.)

Comparison between distorted anger and healthy anger release

Distorted anger: aggressive behavior
- Loud yelling (or no sounds)
- Hurtful and destructive (hitting, biting, kicking, breaking things)
- No tears
- Child does not feel safe
- Does not resolve painful feelings
- Adults need to stop the violence

Healthy anger release: temper tantrum
- Loud crying and screaming
- Active body movements, but no violence or destructiveness
- Tears
- Child feels safe
- Resolves painful feelings
- Adults need to accept the tantrum

This section and the following ones focus on genuine temper tantrums, which represent a healthy release of anger and frustration. Just as with calmer forms of crying, tantrums do not last forever. Children stop of their own accord after they have finished releasing pent-up feelings of frustration and anger. It's important to stay with children during these emotional meltdowns so they will feel loved and accepted.

Many parents find it difficult to tolerate tantrums. You may feel that your child is out of control or falling apart. Perhaps you fear that you have spoiled him by not being firm enough in the past. Maybe you think he is just trying to manipulate you into giving him what he wants. Some people believe that tantrums, willfulness, and stubbornness are bad habits that must be stopped before they grow out of hand. In the past, some people even felt that children who had frequent tantrums were possessed by a demon, and the recommended remedy was to "beat the devil out of the child." Nowadays, your child is more likely to receive a psychiatric diagnosis and be prescribed medication.

If you have any of these mistaken ideas about tantrums, you may think that your job is to discourage your child's meltdowns. Unfortunately, many parenting books offer suggestions for stopping temper tantrums. This advice ranges from ignoring the tantrum to throwing cold water on the child's face. The authors of those books appear to be unaware of the fact that the repeated repression of healthy anger release in children can have negative consequences later on, including depression and aggression.

Why do children cry and rage about insignificant things?

Some temper tantrums seem to be unjustified by the situation that triggers them. For example, a child screams for half an hour because she cannot find a toy or because her favorite cup is in the dishwasher. These examples do not involve any major trauma, yet the children scream as if their very survival has been threatened!

The reason for this type of overreaction is that children use minor pretexts to release accumulated stressful feelings. The lost toy could be a pretext that triggers memories of past losses. The dirty cup could symbolize times in the past when the child's real needs were not met. The child could also be crying about a specific trauma from the past, which is triggered by a current incident. It's therefore important to take your child's reactions seriously, even when they appear to be disproportionate.

Sometimes a child will cry and scream while saying "I can't do it," even though she is fully capable of doing the task (such as taking off a shoe). This behavior sometimes confuses parents because they know that their child is able to take her shoe off. But perhaps she is using the situation to release built-up frustrations resulting from an inability to do *other* things, which really are too difficult.

I use the term "broken cookie phenomenon" to refer to these situations in which children's tears and tantrums appear to be an overreaction to the incident that triggers them. This term stems from an imaginary situation in which a child screams because her parents give her a broken cookie. Anything can act as a tantrum trigger when a child has an overload of stress. Sometimes the trigger resembles the original trauma, but not always. The following example of my own daughter illustrates the "broken cookie phenomenon."

> One day at four years of age, Sarah had two falls: one from a low wall that she was walking on, and one from a trapeze. Her injuries were not serious. I was with her both times, but I did not have much attention for her crying because I was supervising other children at the time. That evening, while preparing for bed, she was sitting on the bathroom counter next to the sink after washing her feet. It was time for her to get down and brush her teeth. Instead, she began to cry, saying, "I can't get down. I might fall." I placed a chair next to the sink, and she easily touched the chair with her toes, but she quickly withdrew her foot and claimed again that she couldn't get down. She continued to cry and say how scared she was of falling. I did not lift her down, because I knew she could easily do it by herself. She screamed and cried for about five minutes while I stayed with her. Then she stopped crying, smiled at me, stepped down from the counter, and calmly began to brush her teeth.

In this example, my daughter's position on the bathroom counter triggered a memory of her falls that had occurred earlier in the day. She used the situation as a pretext to complete the crying that she had not completed at the time. When children have accumulated painful feelings and frustrations, they will make use of any little pretext to cry.

Sometimes a limit will trigger a meltdown. In the following example, a mother described a typical "broken cookie" situation with her six-year-old daughter, triggered by limits that the mother set.

It'll be something that sets her off, like when I say, "No, I'm not going to buy that toy right now." She'll just cry and keep saying, "I want it." I can't reason with her. We get nowhere on the talking level, and she doesn't want me to hug her or anything. After she finally cries it all out, I hug her and then it's okay. I usually realize by then that it's probably just pent-up tension. It isn't about the toy or anything like that. It's just a whole bunch of stuff that she needs to get out. I try to be aware of that.

When your child acts like this, you may feel that she is just trying to manipulate you into buying the toy. However, that is probably not your child's real goal, nor is it her real need. If you give in to her demands and buy the toy, you will probably temporarily placate and calm her. But you may discover that she finds another pretext for a meltdown later in the day. So when you interrupt these tantrums, either by giving in to your child's demands or with punishment, you will probably only postpone the outburst.

Instead of giving in, you can remain firm with your limit while accepting your child's disappointment and anger, even when her reaction appears to be exaggerated. You can calmly say, for example, "I'm not going to buy the toy, but I see that you are really angry about that. I will stay with you until you feel better." Children rage in anger in these situations, not because they are spoiled or manipulative, but because they need to release painful, pent-up emotions, which may have nothing to do with the incident that has triggered the tantrum. Children are like a pressure cooker that needs an escape valve for the steam. After the tantrum, your child will probably become calm and cooperative, and will no longer make unreasonable demands. This peaceful state will last until your child again becomes frustrated or has a build-up of stress.

If I accept my child's tantrums, won't they occur more frequently?

(Reminder: The word "tantrum" in this book refers to a spontaneous rage reaction accompanied by tears, but without any aggression or destructiveness.)

Some parents worry that they will somehow reinforce their children's tantrums if they "reward" the child with attention. However, a tantrum is a physiological discharge process comparable to defecating. When a child has an accumulation of emotional stress, he will feel an urge to release the tension by crying and raging. This process is similar to an urge to defecate when there is an accumulation of feces in his colon. When you accept your child's tantrums, you won't cause him to have more frequent meltdowns, because he will stop raging after he has released all of the accumulated tensions. He will not need to have another tantrum until his frustrations and tensions have again accumulated. To discourage a temper tantrum will lead to emotional constipation: a literal bottling up of feelings.

When you first begin this approach, however, your accepting attitude may result in more tantrums, at least temporarily. The constipation analogy helps to understand this. Some children become constipated and have a bowel movement only every three or four days because of a fear of toilets. After the child overcomes this fear, his bowel movements will return to a more normal pattern and begin to occur more frequently. But you won't cause diarrhea by paying attention to your child when he sits on the toilet! Likewise, if you have punished or ignored your child's tantrums in the past, your child may begin to have more frequent meltdowns after you begin to accept them. It may *look* as if you are reinforcing the behavior and causing tantrums to occur more often, but in reality your child is simply displaying a more normal crying pattern because he now feels safe to express emotions. *Children do not cry or rage any more than they need to.*

If you are still concerned about reinforcing tantrums by paying attention to them, all you need to do is make sure that you also pay attention to your child at times when he is *not* raging. This will help to reassure you that your child is not faking a tantrum just to get your attention. It's actually impossible to fake tears, so if real tears are flowing, your child is definitely releasing tensions.

Children who are raised with this kind of acceptance are typically very open and expressive at home. They do not hesitate to show their raw emotions when they feel safe enough to do so. So be prepared for some intense moments, and try to remain calm through your child's tantrums. The amount of crying and raging will probably decrease as your child grows, but even an eight-year-old may still need to have an occasional meltdown. The frequency and intensity of your child's tantrums will depend on the amount of stress in his life. Don't forget that school can be a major source of stress for some children.

What if my child has a tantrum in public?

You may understandably feel embarrassed when your child has a full-blown meltdown in a supermarket or public playground. As children grow older, they begin to understand that some situations are inappropriate for loud behavior, such as tantrums, and they can learn to control their outbursts. But every child needs to have a safe place to cry and a person who will accept her tears and tantrums. During the early childhood years, children benefit by having contact with such a person on a daily basis.

Some parents worry that allowing tantrums at home will give their child permission to rage everywhere else. But it actually works the other way around, because children who have the freedom to release emotions at home have no need to do so elsewhere. If you wish to have quiet children in public, you cannot expect them to be quiet at home. The more your child can express her feelings openly at home, the more "well-behaved" she will appear to others.

You can try to predict a tantrum by paying close attention to your child's behavior. When she becomes extremely demanding or shows other signs of an imminent meltdown, you can avoid going out, if possible, until the tantrum has occurred. You can even provoke a tantrum by setting a loving limit. This approach is similar to making sure your child uses the toilet before leaving home. When you provide this acceptance of tantrums at home, your child will do most of her crying and raging there and will not feel the need to vent her emotions in public.

Even with this approach, however, your child may still have an occasional outburst in public. When this occurs, there is no need to stop your child's tantrum unless it is disturbing other people. A tantrum in a supermarket or playground can allow you to model an accepting attitude and show other parents that it is not necessary to stop or punish a child at such times.

If you must stop your child's crying or raging in a place where such behavior is disturbing other people, you can take your child to another room and stay with her. If that's not possible (such as on an airplane), you can do your best to calm her down with the use of distractions. When you interrupt a meltdown, however, be aware that your child will probably need to complete it later.

What if children suppress their crying?

When parents lack information about the benefits of crying, some children learn to suppress their crying at an early age. Some parents try to calm their baby down with pacifiers, movement (jiggling, rocking, etc.), frequent nursing, and other distractions, thinking that he will feel better once he stops crying. However, when the crying is for stress release (rather than communication of an immediate need), babies will benefit more from crying in arms as much as needed.

After the first year, parents are often led to believe that their toddler is spoiled or manipulative when he cries or rages. Parents who hold this belief feel that it's their job to stop the crying, and they accomplish this by ignoring or distracting the child. When these methods fail, some parents resort to threats or punishment out of desperation and frustration.

The result of this early repression of crying is that some children reach the age of two years with accumulated painful emotions resulting from earlier stresses and traumas, but with no acceptable outlet for them. These children do not cry very easily because they have learned that it is not safe to do so. Children will do practically anything to gain their parents' love and approval. When parents don't fully accept crying, children typically find ways to suppress their tears.

Some children repress their emotions by sucking on a pacifier or their own thumb. Children who are still being breastfed sometimes acquire the habit of using their mother's breast as a pacifier. They demand frequently to nurse when they are upset, even when they are not hungry. Some resort to overeating, especially if the parents frequently offered a breast or bottle in the past to stop stress-release crying when the baby wasn't really hungry. Another common behavior is to clutch or suck a favorite blanket or toy (sometimes called a security object). Some children tense their muscles to avoid crying, while others resort to self-stimulating behaviors (such as head-banging, self-rocking, or excessive masturbation) to divert themselves from their painful emotions. Those who have access to electronic devices may learn to depend on these forms of entertainment to distract themselves from their feelings.

I call these various suppressing mechanisms "control patterns," because they are patterns of behavior that children use to control emotions. Almost any behavior can become a control pattern if the child uses it to hold feelings in. Typical control patterns in adults include smoking, nail biting, drugs, alcohol, overeating, and muscle tensions.

In a study of behavior problems in normal children, the researchers found that thumb sucking gradually decreased between 21 months and 14 years of age. However, they observed an *increase* in the incidence of nail biting during that same period. In fact, the percentage of nail biters at 14 years of age was similar to the percentage of thumb suckers at 21 months of age (about 25%). As children grow, it seems that they do not lose their control patterns, but simply modify them so they become more socially acceptable.

Children who have learned to repress their crying in these ways often display additional symptoms that indicate repressed emotions. Some become aggressive, hyperactive, oppositional, or demanding, while others have difficulty concentrating. Other symptoms of repressed emotions include anxiety, phobias, nightmares, and sleep disturbances.

Children with these behaviors often receive a psychiatric diagnosis, and many people assume a biological cause and the need for medication. The behaviors that receive the most attention are usually those that are disruptive and difficult for adults to handle (such as hyperactive, oppositional, and aggressive behavior). Before assuming that your child has a biological disorder, however, it's important to search for possible sources of stress or unhealed trauma. Early emotional trauma can affect the structure and function of the brain. We don't know how many of these neurological effects are reversible, but it appears that allowing children to release emotions through crying and raging can help to alleviate these symptoms in some cases. Many parents who have consulted with me have reported (with much relief) that their children's difficult behaviors and sleep problems decreased or completely disappeared after the parents began to implement this approach.

Children who rarely cry and who appear calm, passive, and somewhat detached may be in a chronic state of mild dissociation (psychological numbing). This behavior, caused by unhealed trauma, correlates with emotional problems later on. Unfortunately, these passive children who appear to daydream a lot rarely receive the help they need, because their behavior is not usually disruptive. Some people even assume that the child's trance-like behavior reflects his personality.

How can I help my child regain the ability to cry?

If your child has learned to repress her tears, you can take steps to help her regain the ability to cry. The longer your child has been repressing her emotions, the more difficult it will be to help her recover this natural healing process, but it is never too late. I don't recommend telling your child that she needs to cry. That direct approach could cause your child to become self-conscious and resist crying even more.

You can begin by changing the words you use when your child hurts herself or seems upset for any reason. For example, if she bumps her leg while playing, avoid the temptation to dismiss any pain she might feel. Instead, ask if her leg hurts, and then simply listen. If you stay close and remain attentive, she may feel safe enough to cry a little. Your reaction is important when your child begins to recover the ability to cry, so try to accept her crying even when you don't understand the reason for it.

After you start showing more acceptance of your child's emotions, you may begin to notice "broken cookie" situations when she seems to be overreacting. She may complain angrily that you have served her cereal in the wrong bowl or that the juice is too cold. You soon discover that nothing satisfies her, and she continues to be angry and demanding. If you are in a hurry, you may not want to encourage a full-blown meltdown at that time. But if you have the time, you can welcome your child's angry crying. The bowl or juice is probably not the real issue, so it's okay to set a loving limit on what you are willing to do for her. If your limit triggers a tantrum, that is probably what she needs to do, and you can welcome the outburst.

Other similar meltdowns may begin to occur spontaneously, and this will be a good sign, although it may be a difficult stage to go through. Your child is not falling apart or becoming overly sensitive, nor is she "spoiled" or manipulative. She is simply catching up on crying so she can release a backlog of accumulated painful emotions. Any crying that occurs is a tribute to your good attention, so you can congratulate yourself that she feels emotionally safe with you.

If your child continues to repress her crying after a month or two of your efforts to accept her painful emotions, you can take a look at the repressing methods she uses (control patterns). For example, does she use a pacifier (dummy)? If so, you can explain to her that you don't think she needs it anymore. Some families hold a little ritual to bury the pacifier or put it into the recycle bin, but only with the child's permission and cooperation.

If you are still breastfeeding your child, that's wonderful. However, are you using your breast as a pacifier to calm her down at times when she might need to cry? If so, there is no need to wean your child, but you can experiment with less frequent nursing and more listening. You can also avoid nursing your child to sleep and welcome her crying at naptime and bedtime. You may find that she begins to sleep better at night after a good evening cry in your arms.

Children who awaken frequently at night usually have pent-up stress resulting from insufficient crying.

If your child sucks her thumb, it would be disrespectful to forcefully remove it from her mouth. The goal is to provide sufficient safety so she no longer *needs* to put her thumb in her mouth when she is upset. Give her your full attention when she sucks her thumb and gently touch the hand that is at her mouth to draw her attention to it. Children will spontaneously take their thumb out of their mouth in order to cry when they feel safe enough to do so. If that approach doesn't work, you can try to elicit laughter by playfully sucking on your own thumb or each other's thumbs, or by suggesting activities such as peek-a-boo or hand clapping games.

If your child feels self-conscious about crying, you can suggest that the two of you practice crying together. This activity will probably make both of you laugh, and it will help your child overcome some of her reluctance or embarrassment about crying. Make sure, however, that your child does not feel teased.

If you yourself rarely cry, your child may not feel safe enough to cry with you. Some parents who have consulted with me notice that their children begin to cry more easily after the parents regain the ability to cry (either through therapy or on their own). You might also benefit by exploring your childhood and recalling what your parents did when you cried. If you feel a lump in your throat when you watch a sad movie, let your tears flow instead of holding them back. If you have had a hard day, ask your spouse or a friend to listen to you and let you cry. Anything you can do to increase your own crying will probably help your child feel safer to cry with you. She will sense your new openness to crying, even if she has not seen you cry.

What if I find it difficult to accept my child's crying?

Your child's crying may be hard for you to accept, at least at first. A main reason for this difficulty is probably the fact that you were not allowed to cry and rage as a child. Perhaps your parents punished, distracted, fed, ignored, teased, or threatened you when you cried. If you weren't allowed to cry (and most people weren't), you will naturally find it difficult to empathize with a crying child, because you lacked the role models for this kind of acceptance. So don't blame yourself if you feel impatient, angry, powerless, or anxious when your child cries. You may think that he is trying to manipulate you or purposely irritate you. You may find yourself wanting to yell or even hit your child, as a mother confessed to me in the following example.

> If they are hurt or disappointed by someone else, I can be patient, loving, and calm. But if they are crying or raging at me in disagreement or to get their way, I get tense. These are the times when I lash out in anger. I want things to go smoothly. When I get so angry, the kids aren't getting my focused attention, and then they often react strongly to that. It's hard for me to calm down once this has started, and things dissolve into mutual exchanges of anger and frustration. Eventually we calm down and talk it over, and I apologize. I feel sad after these times. The kids don't always get their self-images mended quickly, and the trust between us is strained.

If your child's crying is deeply disturbing to you, and you fear that you might harm him, a temporary solution may be to distract your child to calm him down. You can suggest a walk, a game, some food, or even some screen time, if necessary. When you use distraction in this manner, however, be aware that your child's crying is probably only postponed. He will still need to finish crying at another time when you (or someone else) has more patience to listen.

If this situation happens more than once or twice, it's likely that you are suffering from unhealed childhood trauma. You will benefit by arranging to have more time away from your child and also by looking for ways to begin your own healing process (through therapy or a support group). You can also create a list of people to call when your child's crying triggers your anger. The more help and support you can find, the less likely you will be to do something hurtful to your child that you will later regret.

Is it okay for me to cry in front of my child?

Many parents have asked me if it's harmful to show their emotions to their children and cry or rage within earshot of them. If you need to cry when you are with your child, it is important to be aware of the manner in which you do this.

It would be an emotional burden for your child to assume the role of counselor or therapist for you. It's unfair to expect children to do this. So if you think that your child might feel responsible for helping you, it would be best to cry away from her, preferably with another adult to support you. If you can't avoid crying in front of your child, be aware that she may become frightened and may need reassurance that you are not falling apart. She needs to know that you are still able to care for her. She may also feel guilty and think that she caused the problem. Even though your child's behavior may have triggered your crying, try to avoid making her feel responsible for your feelings.

Be very cautious with anger, especially distorted expressions of anger such as violence and destructiveness. Your child will probably become frightened if you yell obscenities or slam doors. A child who has been hit or spanked will feel especially terrified. Furthermore, such behavior is not a good role model for your child. If you feel the need to yell or hit, you can do this into a pillow, while reassuring your child that she is not the target of your anger.

With these precautions, there may be some benefit for your child to witness your tears, because she will have a role model of an adult who can express emotions. She will learn that people of all ages need to cry occasionally. Little boys, especially, may benefit from seeing their fathers cry once in a while.

Exercises

Explore your childhood

1. What did your parents usually do when you cried as a child? Did they yell, punish, distract, ignore, or comfort? What words did they use? How did they react when you had a temper tantrum?

2. Did you ever see your parents cry? What were the occasions? How did it make you feel?

3. Do you recall a traumatic event from your childhood that you still need to cry about?

Express your feelings about your child

1. How do you feel when your child cries? What do you feel like doing? (This isn't necessarily what you *should* do.)

2. How do you feel when your child has a temper tantrum?

3. Does your child repress his crying with a control pattern (special blanket, thumb sucking, bottle, etc.)? How do you feel about this behavior?

Nurture yourself

1. Try to become aware of your own control patterns (repressing mechanisms). When you feel stressed, anxious, or depressed, do you distract yourself with social media, food, alcohol, drugs, or other habits? What do you really need at those times?

2. With your spouse or a friend, take turns listening to each other for five or ten minutes each, while you share the upsets of your day. Find someone who is willing to listen to you during emotional upsets. Join a support group or find a therapist who encourages you to cry.

3. Watch a sad movie and allow yourself the freedom of tears.

Chapter 2

Fears and Frights

MOST YOUNG CHILDREN have some fears. Parents often feel concerned about these fears and wonder what to do. This chapter describes different kinds of fears and the various factors that can cause them. It includes recommendations for helping children overcome anxiety and specific phobias. The two final sections cover the topics of nightmares and separation anxiety.

What causes children's fears?

Fears are evident from birth on. Loud noises and sudden movements can easily startle newborn infants. During the second half of the first year, most babies develop separation anxiety and a fear of strangers, which usually indicate a healthy attachment to the parents. These fears normally decrease between two and eight years of ages, but new fears often emerge during those years. Children's fears during early childhood fall into two major categories: developmental and traumatic. Developmental fears result from immaturity, while traumatic fears stem from distressing events.

Developmental fears

Several factors contribute to children's developmental fears. A fear of being alone in the dark may have had survival value in prehistoric times and be wired into children's brains through the process of natural selection. Young children who strongly resisted being left alone at night probably received more protection from their mothers and were therefore less likely to die from exposure to the cold or attack by an animal.

Another factor is lack of information. Many childhood fears arise because of insufficient information or misconceptions. Much of the world appears mysterious, confusing, and unpredictable to young children. In the past, humans probably feared thunder, lightning, eclipses, and other natural events because they had no understanding of the physical laws governing these phenomena. Modern children have fears for similar reasons. Anything that a child does not fully understand can be a source of fear, for example toilets, a wind-up toy, or thunder. Children continually form their own theories about how the world works, but their ideas are sometimes incorrect because of insufficient information. A child might think, "If all of that bathtub water can disappear down that tiny drain, then I could go down the drain too."

Around three years of age, children start to become aware of death and their own mortality. Babies lack a conscious understanding of death, even though they instinctively know what they need in order to survive. But this blissful state changes around the age of three, when children begin to ask questions such as "will I die?" and "why do people die?" This growing awareness of mortality can give rise to new fears. Your child may suddenly resist a story book about monsters that used to be a favorite, or express a fear of ghosts.

A child's growing imagination can further contribute to these developmental fears. The ability to imagine the future increases during the early childhood years. While this cognitive ability is vital for planning ahead and functioning effectively in the world, it can also lead to fears. Children whose imagination can conjure up frightening events may have difficulty distinguishing reality from their own fantasies.

The following example of my daughter illustrates a developmental fear that appeared when she was almost three years old.

When Sarah was little, I used to hold her in my arms in the evening until she fell asleep. One evening, just a few weeks before her third birthday, I was holding her, and she suddenly said, "I don't like the curtains." It seems that she was afraid of the shadows thrown on the curtains from the bushes and the street light outside the window. The shadows looked like huge animals to her. She requested a light in the room, something she had never needed before, even though the curtains and shadows had always been there. About a week after this, she asked her first question about death: "What can dead people do?"

Traumatic fears

As mentioned in Chapter 1, unhealed trauma from infancy can carry over into childhood if the baby lacks opportunities to cry in arms with an adult's loving attention. Some of the lingering effects of early trauma include fears. For example, a child whose mother was hospitalized for a few weeks during the child's first year might have an intense fear of separation when starting preschool at the age of three. A difficult birth could be a child's first major trauma and lead to fears later on. Some psychologists think that claustrophobia (a fear of being in closed spaces) can have its origin in a long birth in which the infant was stuck in the birth canal.

New frightening experiences, such as an accident or a bee sting, can also result in later fears. If your family must evacuate because of a wildfire, your child could acquire a fire phobia (and so could you!). It's impossible to protect children from all distressing experiences, so most children have some traumatic fears.

Children can also acquire fears by association, and these are called conditioned fears. Anything that frightens a child can lead to a later fear of the objects involved or the events occurring at the same time. In a famous experiment done in 1920, an eleven-month-old boy called Albert was happily playing with a white rat. Suddenly, the experimenter struck a suspended steel bar with a hammer to produce a loud, startling noise. The bar was struck a total of seven times while Albert played with the rat. Following this, Albert was terrified of the rat, and he avoided it in fear when he saw it, even though the rat itself had not hurt him. The conditioned fear also spread to other, similar objects, such as a rabbit, dog, fur coat, and cotton wool. The spreading of these kinds of fears to other objects is called *generalization of a conditioned fear response*. For example, if your child is happily playing in a wading pool when a sudden clap of thunder occurs, he may fear the wading pool from then on. This fear of bathing could spread to swimming pools, lakes, or bathtubs.

Your own fears can also frighten your children, and this fact can cause your children to acquire your fears through the process of conditioning. If you see a spider in the house and make a sudden movement or sound, your child may develop a fear of spiders from that incident. He may not initially be frightened by the spider itself, but by *your reaction* to the spider. A parent's sudden fear reaction can terrify children. This fear will then generalize to anything associated with the situation, just as little Albert came to fear rats in the experiment described above. This mechanism of parent/child fear contagion had obvious survival value during human evolution, because children would have been more likely to survive if they could quickly acquire their parents' fears of dangerous places or animals, such as poisonous snakes.

Unfortunately, this mechanism also has disadvantages, because you can pass on unhelpful fears to your child. The following example demonstrates fear contagion with my son.

> At two years of age, Nicky developed a fear of wind because I once overreacted and suddenly became frantic when some important papers of mine started blowing away in our back yard. My reaction must have startled him, because I had suddenly switched from a calm mother to a hysterical one. For several months afterwards, he panicked, screamed, and cried when a sudden gust of wind occurred in our back yard and blew his toys around.

If you feel overly worried about your child's safety, you could unconsciously pass on that anxiety to him. He may become fearful because of you and avoid trying new things or separating from you. It's important to instill a healthy awareness of danger in your child, but you don't want him to suffer from chronic anxiety.

Factors contributing to children's fears

Developmental fears
• Evolution
• Lack of information
• Growing awareness of death
• Child's imagination

Traumatic fears
• Unhealed trauma from infancy
• New traumatic or frightening events
• Conditioning and generalization

What fears are the most common?

Most children between the ages of two and eight years have some fears, and the specific ones they acquire depend on their experiences. In spite of individual differences, however, certain fears are more common than others. The most common early childhood fears (in Western cultures) are of darkness, large animals, snakes, separation from parents, masks, thunderstorms, and imaginary creatures (ghosts, monsters, witches, etc.).

You may wonder how to determine whether your child's fears are developmental or traumatic in origin. This distinction is not always obvious, because some fears could have either cause. For example, a fear of dogs is a common developmental fear, but it can also result from a frightening encounter with a dog. Traumatic fears are obviously more likely when children have had traumatic experiences, especially if the children did not have opportunities for emotional healing. Traumatic fears are usually also more specific, more intense, and more persistent than developmental fears. Children do not easily overcome traumatic fears without some therapeutic intervention, whereas developmental fears usually disappear by themselves as the child matures.

Children differ in their degree of fearfulness. Girls tend to have higher levels of fear and anxiety compared to boys. This difference between the sexes may be caused by the way parents treat daughters compared to sons. Children's inherited temperament can also play a role. For example, 15 to 20% of children (of both sexes) are highly sensitive by nature, and these children become easily overwhelmed and overstimulated. They also tend to have more fears and are typically slow to respond in new situations. Instead of immediately participating in an unfamiliar group activity, your highly sensitive child may act shy, withdrawn, and anxious at first. She may choose to sit on your lap and observe the activity for a long time before she feels ready to join the group.

In most cases, you will probably know when your child is anxious or frightened. She will tell you that she is scared and will try to avoid the feared object or situation. She may show her anxiety by clinging to you or crying. Be aware of less obvious indications of anxiety as well, which can include physical symptoms (nausea, headaches, or stomachaches), sleep disturbances, and thumb sucking.

Fears are not logical and do not respond to reason. Young children typically act terrified of quite harmless things, such as a flushing toilet, while showing no fear whatsoever of real potential threats to their safety, such as a busy street. It's only natural to find this frustrating, especially when your explanations fail to have any effect.

It's important to be aware of your child's fears and consider all possible causes. Although you may feel worried or frustrated about your child's fears, remember that early childhood fears do not necessarily mean that your child is severely disturbed or will suffer from anxiety disorders later in life. Developmental fears between two and eight years of age reflect a normal part of childhood and do not indicate psychopathology, even though fears of similar intensity in adults might be considered pathological.

Sometimes children's fears interfere with their ability to eat, sleep, defecate, play, or learn. This situation is more likely to occur with traumatic fears, but it could also happen with developmental fears, especially in a highly sensitive child. If your child's health and daily life are affected to this extent by her fears, I recommend supplementing the information in this chapter with the advice of a competent professional.

How should I react when my child expresses a fear?

When your child expresses a fear, you may feel tempted to reassure him by telling him that there's nothing to be afraid of. But such a statement, although well-intentioned, denies the reality of your child's feelings. When you tell him to be brave without offering to help him with his emotions, he may feel bad for his inability to control his anxiety, and that's not the goal you had in mind!

The first helpful step is to acknowledge your child's fear while offering empathy and hope. You can say, for example, "I see that you are scared of the ocean. I will figure out a way to help you with your fear so we can enjoy going to the beach again." By saying this, you will let your child know that you understand how he feels and are willing to help him.

Never tease your child for having a fear, and tell your child's siblings and friends not to do so either. Teasing is disrespectful, and it will not make the fear go away. On the contrary, it will only create more painful feelings for your child to cope with. A child who has been teased may choose to keep his fears to himself, but he will not become any less fearful.

You may think that it's helpful to protect your child from the objects or events that frighten him. Perhaps you avoid going to the beach if your child is afraid of the ocean, or stay away from a friend's house if your child is terrified of the dog. Although this protection may be the right thing to do at times, it will probably not help your child overcome his fears. Furthermore, you may eventually become resentful of your child if his fears prevent you from doing what you enjoy (such as going to the beach). You obviously need to shield your child from real threats to his physical safety, but you do not need to protect him from imagined dangers. In the long run, this approach could actually reinforce his fears, because he might think that there must be real danger if you continually avoid those activities.

The other extreme is not any more helpful. You don't need to force your child to confront situations that frighten him. I have seen well-meaning, but misinformed, parents plunge their terrified children into swimming pools or force them to sit on Santa Claus's lap in spite of the children's loud protests. This approach can further terrify your child and lead to resentment and anger.

So begin by acknowledging your child's fear and offering empathy. You won't increase his fear by doing so. All children need to feel understood and accepted, no matter how they are feeling. The next step is to intervene in specific supportive ways, as the following sections describe.

What does research tell us about overcoming fears?

Therapists do not generally treat children's developmental fears, because children normally outgrow them without any interventions. However, there are effective treatments for fears of traumatic origin. The common factor in all successful intervention programs is some kind of exposure to the feared object or experience so the child can become desensitized to it. This approach, called exposure therapy, is based on the idea that repeated exposure to the feared object without any frightening consequences will allow the child to learn that it's harmless. Therapists expose children to feared objects in various ways: gradually (systematic desensitization), more directly (flooding therapy), and symbolically through play (play therapy).

In addition to the fear-reducing effects of repeated exposures, there is evidence that laughter helps to counteract the stress response and reduce anxiety. Laughter therapy is not new. Throughout the ages, shamans, clowns, actors, and court jesters have used laughter intuitively to help people overcome both anxiety and depression.

Therapy with laughter has been found to be effective for children. For example, therapists have successfully used clowns to reduce both anxiety and pain in hospitalized children. Other methods for promoting laughter during therapy with children include exaggeration, nonsense and general silliness, or role playing scenes in which the therapist pretends to be clumsy, stupid, or powerless.

The exposure therapy approach called "systematic desensitization" does not claim to be a method using laughter, but it is possible that laughter occurring spontaneously accounts for at least a part of its effectiveness. The original idea of systematic desensitization was to have the patient gradually imagine a fear-producing stimulus while maintaining a state of relaxation, until the stimulus no longer triggered a fear response. The theory claimed that the stimulus would become associated with relaxation instead of with physiological arousal (that is, fear).

Although systematic desensitization does work in many cases, it is interesting that relaxation is not a necessary factor for its success. Some therapists have discovered that producing laughter with the use of humorous visual images is even more effective than trying to get the patient to relax.

Crying can be helpful as well. In Chapter 1, I described the beneficial effects of crying and raging. These forms of emotional release, often accompanied by trembling, can help children overcome fears. In fact, the exposure therapy approach called "flooding" often involves a strong emotional reaction by the child, with crying and raging. Flooding therapy may be especially useful for situations in which quick results are important for the child's health, for example, if a child's phobias prevent her from eating or sleeping.

In conclusion, some kind of repeated exposure to the feared object or situation is necessary for children to work through their fears. The exposure can be real or symbolic (for example through pictures or through play), and it allows children to become desensitized to the feared object. It appears that healing can be further enhanced when some elements of humor are added, which allows children to laugh while being exposed to the feared stimulus. In some cases, crying may also be beneficial, provided the child feels safe and knows that the situation is not really threatening.

How can I help my child overcome fears?

If your child's fear is developmental (not a result of trauma), giving information may be sufficient, because many developmental fears result from a lack of information. It never hurts to fill in your child's knowledge gaps and correct his misconceptions. The following example (mentioned in the first section of this chapter) returns to my daughter's fear of the curtains at night and describes how providing information solved the problem.

> At age three, when Sarah developed a fear of the curtains at night (because of the large, strange-looking shadows on them), I showed her the street light (the source of light), and the bushes by the window that were casting the shadows. We looked at them and talked about them, both during the daytime and after dark. For several days, she kept pointing out the street light and commenting on it to others in the family. After that, she no longer seemed frightened of the curtains at night and even said, "I like the curtains now."

Children acquire mistaken notions about all sorts of things, and these misconceptions often lead to fears. For example, your child may be terrified of bleeding to death from a scratch, but once he understands about the coagulation of blood, his fear will probably subside. Children need information about their own bodies and about household devices such as toilets and vacuum cleaners. They need to hear correct facts about animals: which ones sometimes attack humans and which do not. They need to understand death and the difference between sleep and death. They also need to know that witches, ghosts, and monsters do not exist, and that nobody has super powers, either good or evil. This information is especially important if the child watches fantasy films or plays video games. Children also need to learn about frightening natural phenomena such as thunder and lightning.

Sometimes information does not help, especially when your child is too young to understand or believe the explanations. Preschool children do not yet have the reasoning ability required to understand all of the cause-and-effect relationships and physical laws that we adults take for granted. A fear of going down the bathtub drain may persist until your child has a clear understanding of the difference between solid and liquid states. You may therefore need to wait for his brain to mature before he can master some fears.

Many fears simply disappear on their own, without any treatment at all, as illustrated in the following example of my son.

> At two years of age, Nicky was afraid to put his beach ball in the neighborhood wading pool for fear it would disappear down the filter drain, an impossible event. No amount of explanations seemed to help this fear subside. When he was seven years old, we returned to our old neighborhood and visited the wading pool, after not having been there for several years. He said, "Remember when I was afraid of my ball going down that drain?" He seemed very amused at the fact that he had once been afraid of such a ridiculous thing.

When information doesn't help, you can try using a playful approach that involves some exposure to the feared object while encouraging laughter. This exposure with laughter can help with both developmental and traumatic fears. You can experiment to find the most effective way to trigger your child's fear while maintaining an atmosphere of fun and safety. The following example illustrates how I used laughter to help my daughter overcome a fear of toilets.

> At three years of age, Sarah was reluctant to use the toilet because of a fear of falling in. On several occasions, I brought a stuffed animal with us into the bathroom, and I playfully made it act as though *it* was terrified of the toilet. This always caused my daughter to laugh a lot. She was usually able to relax and use the toilet after these games, and her fear eventually disappeared.

Children sometimes spontaneously use play to overcome their fears, and they do this through intentional exposure to the feared objects while laughing. I live in Southern California, and I have many opportunities to observe young children at the beach. The ocean must seem an immensely powerful and frightening force to a young child. Children often run a little distance into the water, but as a wave approaches, they quickly run out to avoid being hit by the wave. They usually laugh during this activity. As they grow braver, they gradually venture farther into the water. They are careful to maintain a good balance between fear and safety by not going in too far, but also by not staying too far away. A casual adult observer may think that such games at the beach are mere child's play of little importance, not realizing that the children are busy conquering their fears of the ocean.

Children are often fascinated by the very objects they fear the most. This attraction probably stems from an urge to overcome their anxiety. They know intuitively that their fear needs to be triggered in order to overcome it, but their fear also makes them keep at a safe distance. These two opposing tendencies can result in an interesting approach/avoidance tendency. For example, you might notice that your child is fascinated, but also frightened, by snakes or large spiders at a zoo.

When your child's fear results from a traumatic event, crying may be the most effective way for him to work through it. A mother described how her eight-year-old son overcame a fear of deep water by crying about an event that had happened three years previously.

When Tomas was five years old, I let him take a swimming lesson from someone who was training to become a swim instructor. She was very eager to teach him how to do things in the water. Well, Tomas was flabbergasted when he saw that Olympic-sized pool and realized that the water was too deep for him to stand in. The teacher pressured him to get in, and when he didn't do so, she forcefully carried him into the water. When he said, "I'm ready to get out now," she said, "Oh, no, Tomas. You're not ready to get out," and she kept him in the water against his will. He didn't cry much at the time. It wasn't a safe situation. He did not cry after we got home, either. But it was traumatic enough that he has refused to take swimming lessons since then. Now he's eight years old, and we have been going to a pool frequently, and I could tell from his conversations that he wanted to try new things in the water. But while we were in the water, he didn't want me to teach or even suggest anything. If I would say, "Try this," he would get frustrated or angry with me. One evening, recently, at bedtime, he was talking about how he could go as far as four feet deep, but he couldn't go as far as five feet deep because he wasn't tall enough. I said, "You know how to float, so it really makes no difference how deep the water is." He got upset with me and replied, "It does too. I'm just not tall enough." Then he declared, "I never want to take swimming lessons," and started crying. Fortunately, I was in a frame of mind where I could be relatively objective, but still supportive, and I said something about how the idea of swimming lessons really frightened him because of that experience he had at the age of five. He talked about it and cried about it, saying that he had really been scared, and that he didn't want to do that again. He cried for a total of 15 or 20 minutes about that episode. The next day, we went swimming again, and he said, "Mom, can I go where it's five feet deep?" For the first time, he wanted to go in deep water over his head, and he did! In fact, he enjoyed it so much that he didn't want to get out of the water! Then, the next time we went swimming after that, he started to jump in and dive for pennies and kiss the bottom of the pool!

This example illustrates how a forceful approach can backfire. We risk increasing children's fears when we force them into frightening situations before they are ready and without any sensitivity to their feelings. At five years of age, my son had a wonderful swim teacher who spent the first few lessons getting him to laugh in the pool with silly, playful activities. The teacher never forced him to do anything against his will. My son loved his swimming lessons and quickly learned to swim.

You can help prevent traumatic fears from developing later on if you encourage your child to cry during, or immediately after, a frightening event. It is especially important to encourage spontaneous crying after an accident. Traumatic fears are more likely to develop later on when the natural physiological processes of emotional release (crying and shaking) are blocked at the time of a traumatic event.

To summarize, children cannot overcome their fears by avoiding what is frightening. They must experience the fear (partially, through play, or by talking about it) while at the same time feeling safe. When this balance of attention is achieved, then emotional release in the form of laughter (and sometimes crying and shaking) will occur spontaneously, and the children will overcome their fears. (See Chapter 4 and also my book, *Attachment Play*, for more information on play therapy.)

How to help children overcome fears

• Acknowledge the fear and offer empathy.

• Give information and correct misconceptions.

• Gently trigger the fear through play and encourage laughter.

• Accept the child's crying.

What about fears of unknown origin?

All the examples in the previous section describe specific fears with obvious causes (either developmental or traumatic). For some fears, however, there is no obvious cause. If your child fears monsters, for example, you may wonder where that fear came from and what to do about it. Some fears are symbolic and do not appear to have a direct link with a traumatic event. Whenever it is too difficult or unsafe for a child to focus on the real threat, symbolic fears are likely to develop. A fear of monsters could begin during the parents' divorce, depression, or illness, or following major trauma such as sexual abuse.

Monsters can also become a symbol for any hurtful behavior by adults, such as hitting or yelling. From the child's point of view, parents who act in these ways are indeed behaving like monsters. No parent is perfect, and most of us lose our patience occasionally. Perhaps the universal evil characters found in fairy tales throughout the world (trolls, monsters, witches, etc.) are meaningful to children because they represent the occasional irrational and hurtful behavior of the adults with whom the children live. Children can also develop symbolic fears because of a future anticipated event such as the birth of a sibling or a move to a new home.

If you suspect an underlying cause, you can encourage your child to talk about the issue. Be aware, however, that she may have difficulty verbalizing feelings about the underlying causes. Information about the symbolic fear itself will probably not be effective. You can tell your child that monsters are not real and show her that there are no monsters under the bed, but that information will probably not make her fear go away. In some cases, however, information or reassurance about the underlying issue can help. In the case of divorce, you can reassure your child that you still love her and will not abandon her even though you and your partner have separated.

Symbolic fears can also be developmental, caused by your child's growing awareness of death, even when nothing traumatic or stressful has occurred. In fact, many fears are ultimately rooted in a fear of death. As mentioned earlier in this chapter, your child's growing imagination can further contribute to these symbolic fears.

Luckily, you don't need to know the cause of your child's fear in order to help her. Emotional release can be effective with any fear, no matter how symbolic, whether the origin is traumatic or developmental. If your child does not spontaneously talk or cry about her fear, look for a playful way to trigger it while encouraging laughter. The following example illustrates how I helped my daughter overcome a fear of crocodiles.

At five years of age, my daughter developed a fear of crocodiles in her room. I showed her that there were no crocodiles, but that information did not help at all. She even verbalized this by saying, "I know there aren't any crocodiles in my room, because they need to live in water, but I am still scared." Her fear was so strong at one point that she was afraid to be alone in her room even during the daytime. I decided that she needed help, so I showed her a crocodile puppet one evening and told her it was a baby crocodile that needed to be taken care of. I role-played a frightened baby crocodile and kept her laughing for about 15 minutes. Later on, after I put the puppet away, she spontaneously cried hard for twenty minutes while talking about her fears while I stayed with her. We repeated this crocodile puppet play on several occasions, and her fear gradually subsided.

In this example, I did not understand the underlying reason for my daughter's fear, but the puppet play got her to laugh, which helped to peel away one layer of her fear. After laughing, she was able to cry, which helped her release deeper tensions and anxiety. Until that day, she had been so frozen in fear that she had not been able to release emotions through either laughter or tears. My playful approach provided a balance between her fear and a feeling of safety, which is what allowed her to laugh and cry. Another playful approach would have been to invite her to play the role of a scary crocodile while I pretended to be frightened. This kind of power-reversal game can be very useful for helping children overcome fears.

    Active games or songs that involve freezing or falling typically cause young children to laugh. When you do these activities with your child, you may be helping her overcome a fear of death. A popular English singing game for young children called "Ring

Around the Rosie" originated during the Middle-Ages following a bubonic plague epidemic in London. There are many versions, but one version goes as follows: *Ring round the rosie, a pocketful of posies, Tisha! Tisha! We all fall down!*

The third line in this song may be an imitation of sneezing (one of the first signs of bubonic plague), and the last line probably refers to dying. During this line, all of the singers typically fall onto the floor. This song must have been therapeutic for children who survived the plague but saw hundreds of their friends and relatives die. It provided them with the tension-release mechanism of laughter. Today, children who know nothing of the plague laugh at the end of the song when everyone falls down. Could they be dealing with their fear of death through laughter? Perhaps this therapeutic laughter explains why this song has survived throughout the ages.

Fear of death is almost universal in both children and adults. This fact explains why amusement parks with frightening dark rides and roller coasters are so popular. We laugh on these rides because we are frightened, but we also know that we are safe. After a full day of such laughter, we return home more relaxed and slightly less afraid of our own mortality.

What causes nightmares and night terrors?

Any fear or frightening experience can cause a nightmare, and most young children have occasional ones. Recurring nightmares may have their origin in very early trauma, such as a distressing birth experience or even prenatal trauma. Nightmares are more likely when children have not fully healed from distressing events.

If your child has a nightmare, hold him and let him cry as long as needed. Afterwards, you can invite him to talk about his dream if he wishes to do so. If he is too scared to talk or cry about it, you can try a playful approach with the goal of eliciting laughter. After laughing, he may be ready to tell you his dream and perhaps even cry about it. However, you don't want him to feel that you are making fun of him.

Sometimes a young child will wake up screaming but be totally unaware of his surroundings. This is called a night terror. The child may also utter words or phrases that make little sense and may tremble or make strange movements. It can take a few minutes, or sometimes an hour, before the child begins to respond normally. Some children fall back to sleep without gaining conscious awareness of their surroundings. In either case, the child usually has no memory of the episode in the morning.

Regular nightmares occur during REM (rapid eye movement) sleep, but night terrors occur during deep sleep (also called Delta sleep). Night terrors often occur within an hour or two after the child has fallen asleep. They can be triggered by a need to urinate or by a sudden noise or jolt. During this stage of sleep, some children also get out of bed and walk into another room, with no later memory of the sleepwalking episode.

Night terrors can be frightening because it may seem as if your child is going crazy. You may feel anxious or powerless when he does not recognize you or answer your questions. You can respond to night terrors the same way you would respond to regular nightmares. Hold your child if he lets you, keep him safe, and reassure him, even if he doesn't wake up or respond normally. Allow him to cry and shake in your arms.

Nightmares, night terrors, and sleepwalking are not considered harmful (unless a child accidentally harms himself while sleepwalking). Both nightmares and night terrors may be children's unconscious attempts to work through stressful or traumatic events. The crying and shaking may represent a healthy release and healing process. The intensity of these nighttime crying sessions may result from the fact that the child is releasing raw feelings without any of the inhibitions normally present during his waking hours.

Some children have nightmares and night terrors frequently, while others never experience them at all. These nighttime crying episodes may occur more frequently if there is new stress or overstimulation in your child's life, or if he has not cried much recently. If your child has frequent nightmares or night terrors, look for potentially serious sources of stress such as bullying at school or sexual abuse. I also recommend taking your child to a doctor to rule out possible neurological causes.

What about separation anxiety past the age of two?

Separation anxiety usually begins during the second half of the first year. Babies normally protest loudly when their mother (or other primary caregiver) leaves the room, even when the baby is left with another person. Babies this age have usually formed a strong attachment to the mother and do not have the language or cognitive ability to understand that she will return. All they know is that she is gone. This resistance to separation is a normal stage of development, which usually reaches maximum intensity between eight and eighteen months of age. Researchers and psychologists consider separation anxiety at that age to be one indication of a healthy attachment to the mother (or other primary caregiver).

When strong separation anxiety continues past the age of two years, some parents wonder whether this behavior is still normal and how long it will continue. Separation anxiety in two-year-olds is still very common and normal. Even older children cannot be expected to jump into strangers' arms or feel secure alone in a room. The strong tendency for young children to prefer familiar people and to resist solitude may have had survival value in prehistoric times when human groups needed to stay together for safety. It would have been highly risky for a young child to leave the group and wander off alone, not caring whether her mother could see her.

When left with *familiar* and caring people, however, separation anxiety gradually decreases after two years of age. If a child over two years of age still has strong separation anxiety *even with familiar people*, this behavior may indicate something other than a normal developmental stage. Children this age, unlike infants, possess enough language and cognitive skills to understand that their parents will return. Their distress is therefore not caused by an inability to understand the temporary nature of the separation.

Several possible reasons can account for unusually strong separation anxiety past the age of two. One may be simply a need to cry. If your child continually clings to her mother and refuses to be left with her own father, perhaps she feels that she cannot cry with her mother. Maybe her mother, out of good intentions, frequently distracted her or used her breast as a pacifier to calm her down as an infant when she actually needed to have a good cry (in her mother's arms). Such a child will appear to need the constant presence of her mother, just as some children become attached to stuffed toys, blankets, or a pacifier. These habits (called control patterns) serve as repressing mechanisms to hold in feelings. When a separation from the mother occurs, it may look as if the child is crying about the separation itself, but in reality, she may simply be making use of the situation to release accumulated painful emotions. Children do need their mothers, but a healthy attachment to the mother looks different from the frantic, clinging behavior seen in a child who refuses to stay with anybody else, including her own father.

If you are a mother encountering this situation with your child, it does not mean that she hates her father or needs you all the time. It may simply mean that she has some crying to do and feels freer to cry with her father. Many mothers have consulted with me about this problem, and I usually recommend that they leave the child with the father for short periods of time, even if the child cries and screams. The parents are usually amazed at the results. The child eventually enjoys being left with her father and stops clinging to her mother. The mother enjoys more freedom, and the child's attachment to both parents becomes stronger and healthier. Another benefit is that the child usually becomes more relaxed, more cooperative, and sleeps better after crying with her father.

A second reason for unusually strong separation anxiety past the age of two is the possibility that the child is suffering from an earlier traumatic separation. For example, if you or your child was hospitalized during the child's infancy, any later separation from you may trigger that original trauma. In other words, separation from you triggers a conditioned fear response. Your child will make use of any new separation to complete the crying she needed to do about the earlier separation. If you allow her to do so, she will heal from the earlier trauma. A separation at birth could be the original trauma that gets triggered by later separations, even if it was only for a day or two.

If you think that your child is suffering from earlier separation trauma, she may benefit by being left with someone whom she knows well and trusts, and who will accept her crying. A gradual approach may work best. For example, you can begin by having the person hold your child while you stay nearby and touch her. Then, over a period of several days, you can gradually move farther away and eventually leave the room while the other person holds your child and accepts her crying.

It's also important to look for other possible reasons for strong separation anxiety past the age of two. If your child suddenly resists being left with a familiar caretaker, you should take that reaction seriously and consider the possibility that the person has frightened or abused your child in some way. But don't immediately assume the worst. The cause could be something as innocuous as a new dog in the person's home. Whatever the cause, a sudden resistance to being with someone familiar should be taken seriously.

Your child may suddenly develop a reluctance to go to daycare or school after having separated from you happily on school days for several months. Again, this reaction should be taken seriously and checked into. Perhaps she has been hurt, teased, or rejected by other children at school. Of maybe there is a substitute teacher who is not as attentive or patient as the regular teacher.

Stress at home can also cause a sudden resistance to separation. Perhaps you are experiencing financial or health problems or are going through a divorce. Any time you are stressed, you will probably become temporarily less patient or attentive. The change in your behavior could frighten and confuse your child, and she will fear that any separation will further weaken her connection to you.

A final reason for strong separation anxiety is your own anxiety. In the first section of this chapter, I described how children can catch fears from their parents. If you constantly worry about your child's safety when she is away from you, she may sense your anxiety and refuse to leave you. So what looks like *her* separation anxiety may actually be a reflection of your *own*. If you think that you are passing on your own anxiety to your child, it would be useful to explore the deeper reasons for your anxiety. It's normal to be concerned about your child's safety and survival, but if you are constantly preoccupied and anxious, the reason may be unhealed separation trauma from your past, including the death of a loved one.

If you are not sure of the reason for your child's resistance to separation or don't know how to deal with it, trust your own feelings and inclinations, even if other people accuse you of spoiling your child or being overprotective. Your course of action must make sense to you and be a decision you can live with. If you discover later that you have misjudged a situation with your child, you can always try a different approach another day.

I would like to stress once again the importance of allowing children time to become familiar with new people and situations before leaving them. There are huge individual differences in the amount of time that children need to feel safe in new situations, and all children deserve our patience and understanding. In the following example, a mother expressed how difficult this was for her.

> I basically have this idea that a four-year-old ought to be independent and outgoing, but she's not always like that. I really get uncomfortable when we go someplace, and she hangs back and climbs in my arms or hides behind me. That drives me nuts. I feel like I'm being sucked into this mire of having to do something I'm not in the mood for doing at the moment, like comforting and holding her. Because it's not in my plans, I have very little patience with it. I want her to separate and go off and be happy. But the day when she did separate easily from me at school, I went home and cried!

Even though your children may handle short separations from you quite well, you cannot expect them to handle long separations. The number of days of separation that children can tolerate depends on their age and familiarity with the person with whom you leave them.

Reasons for unusually strong separation anxiety past the age of two
(when the child is left with a *familiar* person)

• The child needs to cry for unrelated reasons.

• The current separation triggers feelings from a previous separation trauma.

• The child has been hurt by the person she is left with.

• The child has been hurt by other children at that location.

• The parent is stressed and less attentive than usual.

• The child senses the parent's separation anxiety.

Exercises

Explore your childhood

1. List the fears you remember having as a child. How did your parents respond?

2. Describe a nightmare you had as a child. How did your parents respond?

3. Were you ever teased for acting frightened? How did it make you feel?

Express your feelings about your child

1. Make a list of your child's fears and try to figure out the causes. How do you feel about them?

2. How do you feel when your child clings to you and refuses to join a group activity (if this occurs)?

3. Do you have chronic fear about your child's safety or survival? Talk about this with a supportive listener, and try to figure out the cause. Is your anxiety related to a loss or traumatic separation from your past?

Nurture yourself

1. Make a list of your own fears and phobias. Focus on one at a time, and make a plan for overcoming it (on your own, or with the help of counseling or therapy).

2. Ask a support person to be with you while you do something that terrifies you (for example, jump into deep water, capture a spider, or ride in an elevator). Allow yourself to laugh and cry.

3. Bring more laughter into your life. See a funny movie or show. Get together with friends that make you laugh. Act silly with your children.

Chapter 3

Living and Learning

CHILDREN'S BRAINS ARE designed to learn, and they do so spontaneously and continuously. This chapter discusses the acquisition of knowledge, appropriate stimulation for young children, and how best to facilitate the learning process. A basic guideline is to think of yourself as a facilitator of learning, rather than an instructor, and to offer your child a rich environment, just as you would prepare your garden for a plant. Play is an important part of the learning process, and this topic is addressed in Chapter 4.

What kinds of experiences are beneficial for young children?

Young children are curious about the world and eager to explore it. They want to learn how the physical world works, how relationships and other people's minds work, what adults do, where things come from, and how to use tools and machines (such as spoons, telephones, and computers). The more children can experience the world, the better they will understand it and figure out their role in it. Your job is to offer your child the kinds of experiences that will facilitate this learning.

During early childhood, children learn best through exploration and real-life experiences rather than formal teaching or screen-based activities. In fact, deliberate instruction can reduce children's tendency to explore and discover things for themselves. Children absorb knowledge through all their senses: by watching, listening, touching, tasting, and smelling, as well as by the feedback from their muscles and inner ears when they move their bodies (proprioceptive and vestibular senses). They also learn by actively interacting with the world, specifically by imitating others, trying to do things (trial and error), manipulating objects, exploring, and asking questions.

After observing, listening, and interacting, children form theories about how the world works, just as scientists do. They learn, for example, that a round block doesn't fit into a square hole, Mommy is not available when she is at the computer, a cat can scratch, snow is cold, and money can buy things. Children's theories are often incorrect at first. A young child might think that ten one-dollar bills are worth more than one ten-dollar bill because there are more of the one-dollar bills. But children continually revise their theories as they assimilate new information and their brains mature. As they grow older, they can also acquire knowledge through books about things that they cannot experience directly.

At first, your child will learn primarily by observing you. Let him participate in as many of your daily activities as possible, such as shopping, cooking, laundry, and cleaning. Include him in your family rituals, traditions, and personal hobbies. If you enjoy gardening, invite him to plant seeds or pull weeds. If your hobby is baking bread, your child can help by measuring and mixing the ingredients. If you celebrate certain holidays with candles, let your child select the correct number of candles. While doing these activities, talk to your child and tell him what you are doing. Try to answer his questions to the best of your ability, even his endless "why" questions. Children's questions are an important way for them to learn.

If your child has the opportunity to watch you learn something new or practice a musical instrument, he will acquire important information about the learning process. He will see that mistakes are part of learning, even for adults, and he will realize that perseverance is necessary for mastering a new skill. However, don't begin a new hobby or activity with the sole purpose of inspiring your child. He will benefit more from seeing you pursue your own genuine interests rather than artificially contrived activities with the goal of educating him. The following example describes how I inspired my children, without realizing it, when I learned to play the accordion.

> I had once expressed an interest in learning to play the accordion, so I was not too surprised when my husband gave me a second-hand one as a present. I had never played one, but was determined to learn. With the help of an instruction manual, I taught myself how to play and eventually became proficient enough to accompany simple folk songs. My children watched me practice, heard my mistakes, and witnessed my perseverance. When my husband brought home a second-hand trumpet, Nicky (age nine) decided that he would learn to play it, and he proceeded to do so (with the help of after-school lessons). Sarah received a small guitar for her sixth birthday, and she, too, had no doubt that she could learn to play it. I showed her a few chords and she soon accompanied herself while singing simple songs. I think that my children's confidence stemmed partly from their observations of me while I learned to play a musical instrument. I practiced the accordion entirely for my own pleasure. I had no intention of teaching my children anything or being a model for them to imitate. (In fact, I sometimes felt guilty about not spending that time with them!) It was only later that I realized the positive effect this had on them.

In addition to learning indirectly from you at home, you can expose your child to the wider world. Most cities offer educational settings such as zoos and museums. Look for the interactive exhibits, which are especially appealing to young children. But don't forget about the educational value of other kinds of activities such as a visit to a train station or airport. Perhaps you can visit the maternity ward of a hospital to see the newborn babies or attend a concert or play. How about a visit to the dump to see what happens to the garbage, or a tour of the water treatment plant? Take your child to a bakery, construction site, factory, or farm. And don't overlook your own work location and those of your friends.

Simple outdoor activities in nature can also offer rich learning experiences for young children, such as wading in a creek, walking in the woods, playing with sand, or making snowballs. If you have opportunities to travel, take your child to mountains, rivers, lakes, forests, deserts, and cities. Let him observe and explore these different environments.

Young children also need to interact with other children so they can make friends and develop social skills. If your child is in daycare or school, or if he has siblings at home, he will gain these experiences. If he does not have these kinds of social opportunities, he will benefit from occasional play dates with other children. Perhaps you can find a family with a child close in age to yours, and take turns with the other parents to look after both children. This arrangement will provide your child with social experiences and also give you occasional breaks from parenting.

As you expose your child to varied experiences, be careful not to overstimulate him. Also, be sure to encourage him to talk about his experiences, ask questions, and re-enact them through play (as described in Chapter 4). These activities will help him to better understand and assimilate the new information.

Should young children be exposed to violence?

We should do whatever we can to protect children from violence. Unfortunately, this is not always possible. Violence is a major source of stress for children who live in homes with domestic violence or in neighborhoods with high crime rates. Children in war-torn countries experience direct violence and witness horrendous scenes, which no child should ever have to endure. Mass shootings and terrorist attacks around the world expose children to frightening and unexpected trauma. Even children who are not directly affected by these events often hear about them or view them on TV news. Exposure to media violence through films and video games can frighten and confuse children and result in desensitization to violence. Furthermore, it teaches children that violence is an acceptable way to solve conflicts.

Another disadvantage of media violence is that it oversimplifies the reasons for violence. Films and video games often portray certain characters as good and others as evil, and the acts of violence are portrayed as being necessary to kill the evil characters before they destroy the good ones. In real life, however, nobody is all good or all evil, and the reasons for violence are numerous and complex. Instead of teaching children to label certain people as evil, we need to teach children to have empathy for everybody and to recognize the underlying reasons for violence. We can explain that people who hurt others are usually feeling powerless and are suffering from childhood experiences of abuse, neglect, humiliation, or oppression.

In an ideal world, children would be protected from all exposure to violence. They would never see people harming each other, either in real life or in the media, and they would know nothing but acceptance, love, gentleness, and respect. But this shielded existence cannot, and should not, last forever. After children have established faith in the goodness of humanity and have a foundation of love and trust, we can gradually tell them about violence and war. To prevent them from feeling overwhelmed, frightened, or discouraged, we can balance this information with explanations about why people hurt each other, and also let them know about peace efforts, including our own.

How can I answer my child's questions about death?

As mentioned in Chapter 2, children become aware of death around the age of three years and begin asking questions about it. You may feel uncomfortable answering your children's questions and wonder how to do so. Perhaps you wish that your children didn't have to learn about such things. The word "death" itself is almost taboo in our culture. Instead, we talk about "putting the dog to sleep" or about the grandmother who "passed away."

Children do not have these inhibitions about death, and their questions reflect an eagerness to learn about it. The directness of your children's questions may shock you: When are you going to die? Will I die? Why do people die? What can dead people do? Do worms eat dead people?

Although I recommend protecting children from witnessing acts of violence (both in real life and in the media), we do not need to shield them from learning about natural death, which is a normal aspect of all biological systems. Children need accurate and concrete information about death, and they deserve to have their questions answered as directly and completely as possible, even though we may feel uncomfortable doing so. The following example illustrates a mother's experience with her son's questions about death.

> As soon as Gary could talk and ask questions, around the age of two-and-a-half, he began to ask questions about death. He was fascinated by dead animals, dead birds, anything. I didn't know how much information to give him, and I was really upset and perplexed about it. I didn't want him to know about all that stuff, and I tried to shield him from it. My concern was that it was awfully morbid, so I would try to change the subject, because his questions were so specific. Then I realized that it was my problem, not his. After that, it became easier for me. I realized that I needed to answer his questions as directly as possible and give him as much information as I could. I got to the point where I could really enjoy telling him about the maggots eating the body of the birds, and dead people too, and what graveyards were for. He wanted to know all the technicalities about disintegrating bodies, how long it takes, and so on. It was one of his earliest preoccupations. He just had to get all that information. Now he's five years old, and he doesn't ask questions like that anymore, because he's got that information.

A good way for children to learn about death is by seeing dead plants and animals. You can casually point out dead insects, snails, and plants, or wait until your child notices them. Small pets, such as fish or mice, provide excellent opportunities to learn about death because they do not usually live very long. If you have buried a pet, don't be surprised if your child expresses a desire to dig up the animal later and look at it! This is her way of gaining information about death and decomposition.

Some children develop misconceptions about death, and these need to be clarified. A common idea is that it hurts to be dead. Children need to know that dead people no longer feel pain. Another confusion concerns death and sleep, so it's important to make a clear distinction between the two. Instead of telling your child about putting a dog to sleep, it is better to say that the vet helped the dog die so it wouldn't have to suffer, and to explain how it was done. Otherwise, your child may develop a fear of falling asleep, thinking she will never wake up again just like the dog.

If a family member or friend has died, you can provide simple, concrete information. If you tell your child that her grandfather has gone to heaven, this will not help her understand what really happened. She needs to know that grandfather is dead and that he can no longer do anything. If you wish to share your religious beliefs with your child, be sure to do so in an age-appropriate manner, because young children can easily misinterpret religious ideas.

If your child asks if you are going to die, this question may reflect a fear of abandonment. One way to answer might be, "Everybody dies eventually, but I don't expect to die for a long, long time." If your child seems extremely preoccupied by the thought of your death, it would be helpful to acknowledge her anxiety and to let her know who would take care of her if you should die.

How can I give my child information about sexuality?

Children typically begin to ask questions about genital differences and reproduction around three years of age. The best way to provide information about sexuality is simply to answer their questions. But first, find out from your child how much he already knows.

It is important to use correct vocabulary when describing genitals and reproductive organs, and to give accurate information. Age-appropriate books can help, but avoid using plants and animals as substitutes for discussing human reproduction. Young children may have difficulty generalizing from plants and animals to human beings. A good way for children to learn about genital differences is to provide natural opportunities for them to see their siblings and their parents naked while bathing or showering.

When your child asks a question, try to avoid giving more information than he needs. If your daughter notices her baby brother's penis and wonders what it is, you can simply say, "That's a penis. All boys have penises." There is no need to offer an extensive explanation of sexuality and reproduction, because she may be interested only in genital differences at the moment.

You can help your child learn where babies come from by providing opportunities to meet a pregnant woman. If you feel comfortable with your child's presence at the birth of a sibling, that experience can also be a wonderful learning opportunity. There is nothing inherently traumatic in witnessing a birth, but you will need to carefully prepare your child for such an event (as described in Chapter 6).

Many parents wonder if it is traumatic for children to see their parents engaged in sexual intercourse. This is a concern especially for parents who let their children sleep in the same room. Most families in Western cultures feel that sexual intercourse should be private, although there are cultures in which sexuality is not hidden from children, with no observable ill effects.

The psychoanalytic literature describes examples of children being traumatized by inadvertently observing their parents engaging in sexual intercourse. However, it is likely that the trauma stems, not from observing the act itself, but from the parents' *reaction* to the child's sudden and unexpected entry into their room. Any anger directed at the child (although understandable from the adult's point of view) can lead to anxiety and guilt in the child, who may then come to associate these painful feelings with sexuality itself.

If your child should happen to see you making love, there is no need to become overly concerned. Make an effort to remain calm and to answer his questions in a straightforward, age-appropriate way. There is no need to offer long explanations. Although you may be irritated, try to avoid making your child feel guilty for interrupting your love-making.

How can I minimize the effect of sexism and gender stereotypes?

In the past, many parents felt responsible for encouraging their children to fit into traditional male and female stereotypes according to their biological gender. The traditional cultural belief was that boys were smarter and more capable than girls, and that girls' primary role in life was to become mothers. Many of the ways that parents and teachers treated children in the past were ultimately based on these two underlying sexist assumptions. However, gender stereotypes such as these are harmful because they prevent children from reaching their full potential.

There is no doubt that boys typically act differently than girls. Boys are generally more aggressive than girls and more likely to enjoy rough-and-tumble play, transportation toys, and building materials such as blocks. Girls, on the other hand, typically engage in more doll and domestic play, art activities, dress-up, and dancing. There are plenty of children who don't fit these stereotypes, but the average trend is in these directions.

You may wonder if the genetic differences between boys and girls determine these gender-typical behaviors and whether or not you can have an influence. Development is always the result of complex interactions between genes and the environment. In the case of sex-typical behavior, research studies have shown that the influence of genetic and hormonal factors is actually quite small compared to environmental factors. So the way you treat your children can definitely influence the degree to which their behavior will conform to cultural gender stereotypes.

I recommend a gender neutral approach, which means offering equal stimulation and opportunities to children of both sexes without making any assumptions about what their interests or abilities will be. A good way to begin is with the kinds of toys you give your child. Be sure to give dolls, toy trucks, and sports equipment to children of both sexes. If your daughter receives mostly dolls from other people, perhaps you can give her a tool kit for her birthday. You can also try to become aware of your attitude. Even though your son has dolls, do you tend to ignore him when he plays with them? Do you encourage your daughter to wear shoes and clothing that are conducive to running and active sports?

Try to be aware of gender biases in children's literature and movies. Many children's books promote gender stereotypes. In traditional picture books, the animal characters are typically all male, with the exception of female animals who are obviously mothers. The male characters in both books and movies usually have the most adventures and take the most risks, while the females are often passive and domestic. With conscious effort, you can counteract these cultural influences by looking for non-sexist literature and movies, and by pointing out gender stereotypes to your child when you encounter them.

The most important factor may be your own behavior, which your child will notice and imitate. Children whose parents have traditional sex roles in the family are more likely to act in gender stereotypical ways. By the time my daughter was three years old, she had already noticed these traditional sex roles in our family, as the following example illustrates.

> When Sarah was three years old, one of her toy trucks was broken. She showed it to me and said, "Papa will fix it." I felt insulted, because she had not even considered the fact that I might be able to fix it. I then realized that I usually left the repairs around the home to my husband, even though I was perfectly capable of learning to repair things myself. So I took my daughter's truck and fixed it!

Gender neutral parenting is difficult to implement because gender stereotypes are so ingrained in our culture. In fact, you may have been shaping your child's behavior since infancy in ways you don't want, without even realizing it. Studies have shown that both mothers and fathers treat their sons differently than their daughters from the day the infants are born. For example, parents typically spend more time talking to their newborn daughters than to their sons, and they handle their sons more roughly than their daughters. They also buy more dolls and domestic toys for their daughters and more transportation toys and sports equipment for their sons. Girls are encouraged to stay close to their mothers and to be pretty and clean. Parents also expect their daughters to be more fearful than their sons. Boys, on the other hand, are expected to be independent and tough, and to keep emotions (such as fear and sadness) to themselves. They are also spanked more frequently than girls and more strongly discouraged from crying. When children need therapy, it's not surprising that boys are usually referred for problems involving anger and aggression, whereas girls are more likely to suffer from fears, shyness, and lack of self-confidence.

Boys and girls who are exposed to these cultural norms quickly learn which toys are culturally acceptable for each sex to play with, and which clothing, tools, and activities go with males or females. Children become aware of these gender stereotypes as early as two years of age. Their personal gender identity forms between two and three years of age, but they don't recognize gender permanence until they are six or seven. When my son was three years old, he asked, "Was I a boy or a girl when I was a baby?" Interestingly, studies have shown that gender awareness and gender identity emerge later in children whose parents have a more gender neutral attitude and approach.

Many parents feel uncomfortable when their child's behavior deviates too much from the cultural stereotypes. Studies have shown that parents are generally more tolerant of these deviations in girls than in boys. Highly sensitive boys and those with older sisters are more likely to deviate from the cultural norm. If your son likes dolls or shows little interest in toy trucks, rough-housing, or ball games, you may need to let go of your fantasies of having a son who excels at sports. Try to ignore other people's comments, and let your son know that it's okay for boys to enjoy typical female activities such as dancing and doll play.

Several clients have asked me if a gender-neutral approach to parenting will influence their child's sexual orientation. There is no evidence that this will occur. In fact, nothing that parents do can influence a child's sexual orientation, which appears to be determined at birth. Children need to know that their parents love and accept them, no matter how gender typical their behavior is, and whatever their sexual orientation turns out to be.

If you would have preferred a child of the opposite sex, you could be putting subtle pressure on her to act in a certain way. I encourage you to explore the underlying reasons why the sex of your child is so important to you. Your child will benefit if you can accept her sex and her interests without any reservations.

In conclusion, gender neutral parenting implies that we offer equal opportunities to children of both sexes and that we treat each child as a unique individual. This approach is the best way to help all children reach their full potential, unhampered by gender stereotypes and limitations.

What can I do at home to help my child become a good learner?

There is no doubt that academic success begins at home. Research has shown that parents have considerable influence on their children's intellectual development and that the home environment plays a crucial role in helping children reach their highest potential. Several factors contribute to this effect.

Parental warmth and responsiveness can increase children's intellectual competence. It is not surprising why this is so. Children who feel secure and loved will not need to focus their attention and energy on meeting their basic emotional needs. They will feel free to explore their environment and have more attention for thinking and learning.

Many people believe that the use of praise is a good way to encourage children to learn and feel good about their accomplishments. Parents and teachers often use expressions such as "good job," "that's a beautiful picture," or "you're a great swimmer." Surprisingly, however, this kind of praise may not be the best way to boost a child's motivation, performance, or self-esteem. Studies have shown that praise with value judgments does not necessarily motivate children to learn. In fact, it can undermine children's intrinsic motivation. Children are born with the desire and the ability to learn, and they naturally take pride in their progress. They don't care whether their accomplishments are "good" or not until we start praising or rewarding them. When we praise or reward children for their accomplishments, they may come to depend on external approval and lose touch with their inherent desire to learn and their natural pride in their abilities.

Another problem is that praise with value judgments can lead to anxiety, insecurity, and low self-esteem. This fact may seem surprising at first, but it's actually quite logical. If we tell a child "you're really smart" when he correctly solves a math problem, he may feel stupid the next time he makes a mistake. In fact, he may become anxious or insecure while doing math for fear of not meeting our expectations about his intelligence.

Instead of offering value judgments about your child's performance or ability ("that was very good"), you can be more helpful by providing other kinds of encouragement. For example, if your child successfully completes a puzzle, mirror his pride and say enthusiastically, "You did it!" or "Wow! That's the hardest puzzle you've ever done." If your child shows you a drawing, ask him to tell you about it. You could also comment on the different colors he used or describe how it makes you feel. Children benefit from having their accomplishments acknowledged, but not judged.

Parental discipline techniques have a huge impact on children's intellectual development. Harsh authoritarian discipline can damage children's ability to think and learn. On the other hand, children's thinking skills are enhanced when parents avoid the use of punishment, offer explanations for restrictions, and invite children to help solve conflicts.

The presence of stimulating materials and activities in the home is another important factor. Children who come from stimulating home environments score higher on tests of mental abilities than children whose homes lack stimulation. For example, the number of books in the home correlates with later academic achievement. (See the next section for more tips on helping your child learn to read.) Provide your child with games and toys that inspire him to imagine, build, create, and think. Music and conversation are also important. Encourage your child to talk, ask questions, and think.

When your child asks a "why" question, try to find out what he thinks before you give an answer. Encourage him to ponder hypothetical situations, such as what would happen if it never rained again.

Your expectations can affect your child's competence. If they are too high, he may feel like a failure when he can't meet them. So try to have age-appropriate expectations and arrange situations that allow for maximum success rather than failure. If your child is struggling with a puzzle that is obviously too difficult, you can offer him an easier one. On the other hand, you don't want to have expectations that are too low. If you continue to help your child get dressed months after he is able to dress himself, he may begin to feel incompetent.

Even with realistic expectations, however, your child will still experience occasional frustrations. You can enhance your child's competence and confidence by helping him cope with these inevitable frustrations, which are an integral part of the learning process. When he feels frustrated while struggling to accomplish something, offer empathy and encourage him to express his emotions. He may need to vent frustrations by crying or raging (as described in Chapter 1). Accumulated, unexpressed frustrations can make it difficult for children to think and can decrease their self-confidence.

In the following example, a mother reported to me how crying helped her child master a frustrating learning situation.

> My daughter, age six-and-a-half, was having a difficult time playing two piano pieces by heart and keeping them separate. Finally, she just started crying and said she couldn't do it. I let her cry while holding her in my arms (for perhaps five minutes solid), and we hardly spoke at all. After crying, she wanted to try again, and she was able to remember the two pieces and keep them separate! She never had a problem with them from that time on.

The following example describes a three-year-old boy's reluctance to dress himself, possibly because his parents had always helped him. His father described to me how he helped his son overcome his feelings of incompetence by encouraging the boy to dress himself and by accepting his emotions.

> He claimed that he couldn't put his shirt on by himself, and began crying. I noticed that he was holding the shirt over his head without really trying to put it on. I was sure he could do it by himself, so I refrained from helping him, but offered encouragement for him to try. He cried hard for about 15 minutes and then easily put his shirt on! He was very proud of himself, and he joyfully took it off and put it back on again several times to show off and practice his new skill.

As your child grows older and encounters structured learning situations in school, as well as homework, he will experience new sources of frustration and discouragement. You can continue to support him by listening to his emotions with empathy.

Factors that help children become competent learners

- Parental warmth and responsiveness

- Encouragement instead of praise or rewards

- Non-punitive discipline

- Stimulating environment

- Age-appropriate expectations

- Acceptance of crying when frustrations occur

How can I help my child learn to read?

Most children learn to talk effortlessly, without any instruction. All we need to do is talk to them, and they figure out by themselves how to pronounce words and combine them into grammatically correct sentences in order to communicate. Learning to read, however, requires more effort and sometimes more deliberate instruction. Remember that our species invented reading and writing relatively recently, long after spoken language evolved, so the ability to read is probably not programmed into children's brains in the same way as the ability to talk.

Studies have shown that parents can play a major role in helping children learn to read. In addition to the suggestions in the preceding section, one of the most important things you can do is read to your child. The more you read to her, the more she will learn to enjoy books and become aware of the connection between printed words and their meaning. Reading to her will also help develop her vocabulary, imagination, and memory, while the closeness and shared enjoyment of books will strengthen your connection with her.

Most children enjoy books about familiar topics. If you take your child on a boat ride, she will probably like books about boats. After a visit to a zoo, select stories about animals. Be aware that some stories or illustrations in children's fiction books can frighten a child who is highly sensitive or very young. Some of the traditional fairy tales can be especially terrifying, so you might want to save those books until your child is a year or two older.

You can also use books to expand your child's horizon, and there is no need to limit your selection to fiction. Look for books of art, science, jokes, biographies, history, and any nonfiction topic that might spark your child's interest. If you and your child enjoy exploring the world of books together, she will naturally want to learn to read.

You can also help your child notice other uses for written language, such as food recipes, catalogs, games, store and road signs, the Internet, and personal communication (letters, postcards, email, and texting). Some parents place written labels on drawers and toy containers to stimulate their children's word recognition skills. Be sure to let your child see you reading to yourself. She will naturally want to imitate you.

Singing songs and playing word games can also enhance children's reading skills. Exposure to rhyming words in songs, poems, and stories will help your child learn to identify speech sounds (phonological awareness), which is an important pre-reading skill. Activities involving alliteration can also help with this skill, for example, creating sentences in which most of the words begin with the same sound ("Sally sells sea shells by the sea shore"). Another alliteration game involves naming all the visible objects beginning with the same sound. During your child's bath, for example, ask her to find objects in the bathroom beginning with the letter T (toilet, towel, toy, tub, toothbrush, and tooth paste). Avoid turning these activities into structured teaching situations. Children learn best through play, so the goal of any pre-reading activity should be to have fun.

With this degree of exposure to written language and speech sounds, some children learn to read without any instruction. They typically begin by trying to read road signs or simple story books that they know by heart. When your child first attempts to read, help her if she requests your assistance, but don't push her.

Most children, however, don't pick up reading easily on their own and need more help. If your child has trouble learning to read, she may receive a diagnosis of dyslexia. This term also applies to children who have mastered the mechanics of reading but can't easily grasp the meaning. Sometimes late readers simply need more time for the necessary cognitive skills to develop, and these children master reading with no problem when they are older. When dyslexia runs in families, the hereditary neurological factor appears to be related to difficulties in rapid auditory processing and phonological awareness.

Sometimes the problem stems from a learning style that is incompatible with traditional instruction. Children who fail to learn with the usual classroom methods can benefit from intervention programs based on their particular learning style. A child with strong visual/spatial skills may learn to read with the help of pictures and visualization, while a child who learns best through touch or movement may benefit from tracing sand paper letters with her finger.

The following symptoms could indicate that your child is struggling in school: headaches, nervous tics, anxiety, disruptive behavior, aggressiveness, stubbornness, and more tantrums than usual. She may say that she dislikes school or her teacher. Ideally, teachers should know how to meet all children's needs, but some schools lack the resources to help children who need special attention. If your child is struggling in school and not getting the support she needs, look for a private tutor or a method that you can use at home. Try to prevent her from feeling stupid. Her reading difficulties probably have nothing to do with her intelligence. In fact, many famous and successful people had trouble learning to read. With appropriate intervention and support, most children can become fluent readers.

What kind of school is best for young children?

There are several principles of learning to keep in mind when selecting a school for your child. The learning style of children under eight years of age is quite different from that of older children and adults. First of all, young children learn best when the learning activities arise from their own curiosity and interests. They also need hands-on experiences with concrete materials before they can acquire more abstract knowledge. Concept formation arises naturally out of concrete experiences. This is especially true for logical, mathematical, and scientific concepts. In addition, play is the primary mode of learning for the first eight to ten years. Finally, appropriate stimulation is important.

The best kind of school for young children is one in which children can learn through self-initiated, play-based activities in a stimulating environment. Young children are not ready for formal, structured teaching or for long periods of sitting. Attempts to impose this on them can result in resentment, frustration, boredom, loss of motivation, or feelings of incompetence. Homework is not necessary. In fact, studies have shown that homework has no educational benefits for children below ten years of age.

Instead of trying to fill children up with knowledge, good teachers provide a stimulating environment and encourage children to ask questions, while providing gentle guidance to help them learn by discovery. This approach is called guided play or guided discovery. The teachers monitor the children's progress by observations and do not administer tests. Direct, deliberate teaching is appropriate when teachers must convey safety instructions (for example, what to do in the case of a fire). But otherwise, it is best if the teachers act more as facilitators and guides rather than instructors.

Another problem with structured teaching is that it usually fragments knowledge into units that are meaningless to young children. In traditional schools, the teachers typically teach reading, writing, and arithmetic as isolated topics with no relation to the children's interests or the real world. Children learn more effectively when they can acquire these basic academic skills in the context of meaningful, real-life projects.

By seven or eight years of age, children are ready to master knowledge and skills in a more structured and systematic way with the help of deliberate teaching, respectful feedback, and regular practice. In fact, children often strive for mastery during middle childhood and enjoy keeping track of their progress, whether it's memorizing the multiplication tables, playing the piano, or becoming proficient at a sport.

Most schools for young children up to age five incorporate these basic principles. Unfortunately, many educators think that a hands-on, play-based approach is no longer necessary for children over five or six years of age, which is the age when public education begins in many countries. The philosophy of typical public schools is that children over five or six years of age must be told what and how to learn. Periods of play are no longer considered essential to the learning process and are often reduced to short periods of recess. These educators think of children as empty, passive vessels to be filled with knowledge.

Based on the most recent research about how children learn, the U.S. National Association for the Education of Young Children has published guidelines for the type of schooling that would be most beneficial for children up to eight years of age. They recommend providing an integrated curriculum with projects and learning centers that reflect children's interests, and exposing children to reading, writing, and arithmetic in the context of these activities (rather than as isolated subjects). This approach is called project-based learning. Art, music, movement, woodworking, dance, and drama are considered to be important parts of the curriculum. Children should be allowed to express themselves freely in these media rather than follow specific directions.

They also recommend plenty of opportunities for play, social interaction, hands-on activities, and learning by discovery. In an ideal school, teachers would find ways to set limits and encourage cooperation without the use of rewards or punishments. Judging children's learning and work by means of letter or numerical grades is considered inappropriate. The guidelines also emphasize the importance of taking each child's individual learning style and rate into account.

Some public schools incorporate these guidelines in classrooms for children up to age eight, but many do not. Increasing numbers of parents in the U.S. and other countries have chosen to homeschool their children instead of sending them to school. These parents, uncomfortable with the educational practices of public schools, provide their children with enriching experiences at home. Homeschooling is legal in many areas, and there is evidence that a stimulating home environment, responsive to children's needs, can produce highly skilled and competent children.

What is the effect of screen-based activities on young children?

In the past, the only screen device in most homes was a TV set. Now we have access to a large variety of electronic devices and screen-based activities. Some provide entertainment, while others are marketed as educational.

Based on what we know about how young children learn, my recommendation is to avoid all screen-based activities for children under seven or eight years of age, for both entertainment and educational purposes. As mentioned earlier in this chapter, young children learn best through movement, hands-on experiences with concrete objects, and live interactions with other people. Screen-based activities during early childhood reduce the amount of time that children spend in more developmentally appropriate activities such as running, jumping, climbing, building, drawing, talking, asking questions, imitating, playing with others, and engaging in fantasy play. Your child might even benefit more from an argument with a sibling than from any screen-based activity, no matter how educational it is supposed to be!

Rather than offer your child an electronic math learning activity, ask her to count out the money needed to buy something. As a better alternative to a computer art activity, give your child real crayons and paper. Instead of electronic games designed to enhance your child's vocabulary, spend more time talking and reading to her. Don't underestimate your importance. You may feel that you have little to offer compared to the sophisticated electronic activities available. But a simple cooking project with your child will provide her with a much richer educational experience than any electronic game you could buy. After eight years of age, your child will benefit more from the educational activities available in electronic format.

Nobody knows the lifelong impact of screen-based activities beginning early in life. We know that neural pathways and connections are created and reinforced in the brain according to how it is used. Experiences early in life literally change how the brain will function later on. So children who engage in lots of screen-based activities early in life will have brains as adults that function differently than those of people who have not had these early experiences.

Research studies have indicated some possible drawbacks from children's screen use. The more time children spend on screen-based activities, the lower their attention span and the lower their academic achievement. There is also evidence that daily and prolonged video game playing over a three-year period during middle childhood and adolescence can change children's brains in ways that negatively impact some cognitive skills, especially verbal abilities.

Another drawback is that many films and video games contain violence. Researchers have known for decades that viewing a violent film can increase aggressive behavior in children. Video games have a similar effect. Studies have found that violent video game exposure results in more aggressive behavior, more desensitization to violence, and less empathy for others. Rather than let children produce violent scenes with a flick of a finger or a verbal command, we need to help them maintain their natural outrage and revulsion at the sight of violence.

The only immediate benefits of screen-based activities appear to be mild improvement of some visual-spatial skills from playing video games, as well as some benefits from viewing educational shows or videos (but not entertainment shows or videos), especially for low-income children. But aside from these findings, there is no evidence that screen-based activities have any educational value for children below eight years of age.

I realize that my recommendation may be unrealistic for many parents. You may feel tempted to keep your child occupied with electronic devices to gain some uninterrupted free time. There is no need to feel guilty if you have done so. But if your child becomes too dependent on these devices, her development could suffer. You might benefit from looking for other ways to meet your own needs and have time for yourself. Would some playdough keep your child happily occupied for half an hour? Can you exchange childcare with a neighbor?

Starting around five or six years of age, your child may begin to feel pressure from friends to play video games or watch certain shows. This social pressure is more likely to occur with boys than with girls, and it could make your child feel left out. He and his friends may not understand why you don't allow electronic devices. Rigid restriction of all screen activities may not be the best solution in this case. If you decide that your child would benefit socially by having some screen time, be sure also to encourage plenty of active playtimes away from screens, as well as interactive and creative projects. If your child's school uses educational electronic devices, you will have no control over that exposure, but you can strive to create a balance at home with active playtimes, as described above.

You may find it useful to become aware of your own screen use. If you yourself pick up an electronic device every few minutes to message your friends, check your email, browse social media, play games, or watch videos, your children will naturally think that screen use is an acceptable way to spend time. Consider discussing screen use with your child and perhaps designating one or two days a week with no screen time for anyone in the family (except for necessary communication). You can plan special family activities for those screen-free days.

Exercises

Explore your childhood

1. Were you pushed to excel academically or musically? How did it make you feel?

2. Did your parents provide you with interesting learning experiences? What did they do that was helpful or not helpful?

3. Describe one or two of the most enjoyable learning experiences you had as a child (in or out of school).

Express your feelings about your child

1. How do you feel about your child's current intellectual abilities or school achievement?

2. Do you feel tempted to push your child academically or musically? Do you have a preference about your child's future career? How would you feel if your child ends up with a totally different career from the one you have in mind?

3. How do you feel about the influence of gender stereotypes on your child? Does your child's behavior conform to, or deviate from, cultural gender stereotypes? How do you feel about that?

4. How do you feel about your child's screen-based activities? Do you wish your child would spend more time doing other things? Do you benefit from the free time that your child's screen use gives you? Is there another way that you can gain some free time?

Nurture yourself

1. Begin a hobby or learn a new skill.

2. Do the adults in your family have traditional gender roles? If so, is there an activity you could do to break these stereotypes (for example, learn to fix something if you are a woman, or learn to bake a cake if you are a man)?

3. How do you feel about your own screen use? Are you a good role model for your child? If not, try to limit your screen use when you are with your child. Find non-screen activities that will nurture you and also serve as a better role model for your child (for example, painting, doing yoga, gardening, or playing a musical instrument).

Chapter 4

Playing and Pretending

THIS CHAPTER DISCUSSES play, one of the most important activities of early childhood. The learning process would be incomplete without play, which allows children to develop new skills and knowledge, and also to assimilate and integrate their experiences. This chapter also describes the therapeutic function of play, with recommendations for specific kinds of parent/child play.

What and how do children learn through play?

Most people recognize play as an important childhood activity, but not everyone realizes that play is much more than just having fun. Play has several functions, both educational and therapeutic. A major function of play is that it helps children learn. In fact, play is the primary means of learning during early childhood. The various kinds of play can enhance children's physical, cognitive, and social skills, as well as their imagination, creativity, and assimilation of information.

The development of physical skills occurs through active play. When given the space and freedom to play, healthy children will spontaneously run, jump, and climb. These activities help to improve their coordination, dexterity, strength, balance, and endurance. Well-designed playground equipment can further enhance these motor skills. Rough-and-tumble play also has an important function. Human children and the young of several other mammals typically engage in this sort of play, usually with their siblings. In addition to the physical benefits, this playful wrestling is associated with better social competence in human children later on.

Children can also acquire cognitive skills through play. In fact, many mathematical and logical concepts have their origin in children's self-initiated actions of grouping, sorting, ordering, stacking, and nesting objects of various sizes and shapes. Play with puzzles, blocks, and other building materials helps children learn to compare and categorize, while enhancing spatial skills and an understanding of mechanical engineering principles. Board games and card games can develop children's reasoning, memory, counting, reading, and spatial skills. These games also provide experiences with cooperation, rules, taking turns, decision-making, probabilities, and logical concepts such as "if-then." Children enjoy exercising their logical thinking abilities and often invent their own games and rules.

Free play can help children's problem-solving ability. In a famous experiment from the 1970's, researchers demonstrated the importance of manipulative free play. They presented three- to five-year-old children with a practical problem of fishing out a toy from a box that was out of reach. To solve the problem, the children had to clamp two sticks together to create a pole long enough to reach the toy. Beforehand, some of the children received different types of training. One group was shown how to clamp two sticks together, another group was given practice in fastening clamps on single sticks, and a third group watched the experimenter successfully perform the task. A fourth group was not given any training at all, but was simply allowed to play freely with the materials before being presented with the task.

The results were very interesting. The children who played freely with the materials solved the task as well as the children who watched the experimenter carry out the task, and they did *better* than any of the groups who had received training. The researchers also observed that the children who had been allowed to play freely with the materials were able to resist frustration better than children in the other groups. They did not give up, even when their first attempts failed, but persisted until they had solved the problem and reached the toy. This experiment shows that children can learn while playing, without any instruction at all.

Young children typically enjoy pretending and creating imaginary scenarios. This fantasy play appears to be a uniquely human activity. From about eighteen months of age, children have the ability to imagine one object representing another. You may notice one day that your child moves a block along the floor, pretending that it's a cat, while saying "meow." This is the beginning of an important stage of development, which the Swiss psychologist, Piaget, called the stage of symbolic thought. As children grow older, their symbolic fantasy play becomes increasingly complex. This kind of play prepares the brain for later abstract symbolic thought while enhancing creativity. Research has also shown that fantasy play with other children (socio-dramatic play) improves language and social skills, because children learn how to form agreements and must figure out how to cope with ideas different from their own.

Children's fantasy play has another important function. It can help children understand and assimilate information. Chapter 3 describes sources of stimulation and information, but receiving input to the senses is only part of the learning process, which is comparable to eating and digestion. When we eat, we first chew and swallow, but our bodies must then digest the food and eliminate waste products. During the learning process, we first take in information, but then we must process it, categorize it, and store relevant parts in a meaningful form for later use.

Adults "digest" new information primarily by talking and writing. In fact, a helpful way to understand and remember new information is to explain it to someone else. By doing so, we organize the information, extract what is meaningful, and relate it to what we already know. Children also benefit by talking about their experiences. But the primary method for assimilating new information during early childhood is by actively reconstructing their experiences with their bodies or through the use of symbolic materials.

A child who rides in an airplane may later pretend to be an

airplane, draw a picture of one, or make one out of paper. A child who attends a wedding is likely to re-enact a make-believe wedding at home and dress up as a bride or groom. When children set up a pretend store, they are actively attempting to understand the function of money. A child who builds a city out of blocks is assimilating information about urban living, city planning, and architecture. When children actively reproduce their experiences through this kind of fantasy play, they are thinking, remembering, making decisions about what is meaningful, putting related facts together, fitting everything into their mental models of reality, and storing relevant facts in memory for later use. This is the essence of learning.

Children have different preferred modalities for their fantasy play. Some tend to use their whole bodies, while others prefer to build, draw, or use toys as props. My son's preferred method for assimilating information was to build three-dimensional models. After a boat trip to an island at the age of five, he built a model of the boat and the island out of cardboard, and taped them to a blue background representing the ocean. My daughter's way of assimilating information was more through the use of physical movements with her entire body. After a visit to Sea World (at the age of four) where she saw whales and dolphins diving into the water, she pretended to be a whale for several days and dived into any bed that was available!

Some play is more imitative and realistic as children attempt to reproduce adult activities. When children first begin to imitate adults, their play is often crude and lacking in details. A two-year-old may pretend to create a shopping list (just like his parents) by scribbling on a piece of paper. This degree of imitation will be sufficient for him at that stage, and he may even insist on taking his own shopping list to the grocery store. A child who has observed people play and sing at the piano from a music book may sit at the piano, bang the keys, sing, and turn the pages of the music book from time to time. These preliminary stages of imitative play are important because the children are creating frameworks into which later learning and details will fit. There is no need to push children to improve their imitations, because they cannot assimilate everything at once.

Although fantasy and imitative play do not occur as frequently after eight years of age, these activities do not totally disappear. The play becomes transformed so that it looks less like play and more like real life or what we call "work," as the following example illustrates.

My son attended an alternative, play-based school between the ages of five and ten years. Children of all ages shared the same classroom and engaged in free play most of the time. Over the years, Nicky and his friends enjoyed creating imaginary restaurants. As a frequent helper at the school, I was able to observe how the activity progressed as he and his friends grew older. At first, the children set up a simple restaurant and sold imaginary food made of paper in exchange for pretend money. They did not worry about the exact amount: they exchanged one piece of food for one piece of paper money. Later on, they began to offer a written menu with a list of foods and prices. They created more elaborate money with bills of different denominations, and they even gave change, as needed. By the time my son was ten years old, he and his friends arranged with the teacher to have a restaurant for the younger children consisting of *real* food. They created a shopping list, bought the food during a field trip to a grocery store, and cooked and served a real meal in the classroom. Their menu listed the food items and prices, and they prepared bills indicating how much each child owed. The only play element was that they still used pretend money (because of a school rule banning the use of real money in the classroom).

In this example, the children practiced arithmetic and writing skills while learning about money, restaurant management, meal-planning, and cooking. They also learned to cooperate toward a common goal. It shows that there is no distinct dividing line between children's play and adult reality. As children grow older, their fantasy play gradually merges with reality until it becomes that reality. In foraging societies, where the children play at adult activities such as hunting or digging for edible roots, this gradual progression from play to real life is the natural sequence of events.

What kinds of play are therapeutic?

In addition to helping children learn and assimilate information, play can also be therapeutic. As explained in Chapter 2, children sometimes spontaneously use play with laughter to conquer their fears. When a child has been injured or has experienced a loss, frustration, or frightening event, her fantasy play will include elements of the experience. This symbolic play will help her figure out what happened and gain some degree of control by changing the outcome. She can compensate symbolically for losses, mistakes, and failures in real life. The play can also offer opportunities for her to talk and laugh, especially if there is an attentive observer. Solitary play is not as effective as playing in the presence of a supportive observer.

Research has shown that parents can be effective play therapists for their children. If your child has experienced a traumatic event, provide toys or props related to the trauma, and encourage your child to play with them while you offer warmth and support. This symbolic play will be especially helpful if your child is unable to talk or cry about the event. By playing with the props, your child can face what happened while feeling safe and can work through the feelings. The following example of my son illustrates the effectiveness of symbolic play following a traumatic event.

> We were having a family outing at the beach, and I announced that I was going to walk to the bathroom. I assumed that Nicky, then two-and-a-half years old, would stay with the others. They were busy talking, and neither they nor I noticed when he started following me. As I returned from the bathroom and walked back to join the others, I found my very frightened and crying little boy

looking for me, while some strangers tried to help him. He had not caught up with me and could not find his way back to the others. I held him and let him cry. However, I was unable to give him my full attention because I was angry with my family for not watching him properly. A few days later, I suggested going to the same beach again, but he adamantly refused. I realized that he still had some unhealed painful feelings from the experience. I held him on my lap and asked him if he wanted to talk about what had happened, but he did not want to talk about it. I was hoping that he would talk and maybe cry some more about the traumatic incident, but he didn't do so. I then decided to try symbolic play. I gathered together some toys (small figures and a small house) and suggested that we pretend the living room rug was the beach. He immediately and eagerly joined me in this activity, and we proceeded to act out together the whole traumatic event. He wanted to play it over and over again. He then changed it to the way he had originally intended. In his altered version, he did not get lost, but caught up with me, and together we went to the bathroom. He enjoyed adding props and more variations and details (trees, boats, more figures), and he talked and laughed while re-enacting the scene. He continued playing the "beach game" for several days until he grew bored with it. A few weeks later, I suggested going to that same beach again, and he was eager to go.

The three major functions of play

- Acquisition of physical, cognitive, and social skills

- Assimilation of information

- Healing from traumatic experiences

The following example illustrates how children can combine all three functions of play in a single play episode.

When my daughter was four years old and my son nine years old, I was hospitalized suddenly for an emergency appendectomy. They were allowed to visit me in the hospital, but the experience was nevertheless frightening for them. For about a week after my return home, they turned our entire home into a pretend hospital, complete with an admitting office, surgery room, recovery room, regular hospital room, and hospital kitchen. Any willing visitor or family member was eagerly admitted to the "hospital" as a patient. The children took their medical histories, performed surgeries, prepared and served imaginary meals, administered medicine, and wrote prescriptions. This play was accompanied by much animated talking and laughter.

During this play, my children exercised their writing, thinking, planning, language, and social skills. They also assimilated information about hospitals, illness, health, and medical intervention. Finally, their play helped them overcome the frightening experience of my hospitalization. When we realize the importance of play and recognize its various functions, it becomes obvious that children make good use of their time!

What is the meaning of imaginary playmates and superhero fantasies?

More than half of all young children create imaginary playmates with whom that speak and interact. These make-believe companions usually appear around two to three years of age and can last for several years. Some children create entire families or populations of invisible creatures. This is a normal stage of development and not a cause for concern. Children with imaginary playmates are usually well-adjusted and mentally healthy. In fact, there is evidence that they are better at understanding how other people's minds work than children who do not have imaginary playmates. Some children do not use their imagination in this way, but that is no cause for worry either. If your child seems generally happy, healthy, and active, and enjoys playing with other children, there is no need to worry about the presence or absence of imaginary playmates.

Just like symbolic play with real props, invisible playmates can help children understand the world, gain control over it, and conquer their fears, as the following example illustrates.

> At four years of age, my daughter, Sarah, had two invisible babies, a boy and a girl. She fed them, put them to bed, and gave them birthday parties. Sometimes they were one or two years old, sometimes three or four, and sometimes "teenagers." Whenever we went somewhere, one or both of her babies would come along, with Sarah holding her hand. At times, Sarah was too busy to take care of her babies, so she would ask someone else to do so. One day, she announced that her baby girl was all grown up and dead. Sarah said, "She's lying on the floor and can't move, and her heart isn't beating, so she must be dead. Now I only have one baby left." The next day, she had two babies again.

In this example, my daughter created imaginary beings, which helped her assimilate concepts of growth, dependency, life, and death. Because her babies were not real, she was free to explore even the most frightening topics (death) while maintaining control over the situation.

Superhero fantasy play is also common during early childhood. The child pretends to be a well-known, powerful hero, such as Superman, or he creates his own magical character. This activity allows him to explore concepts of power and superhuman abilities such as x-ray vision, mental telepathy, superior strength, or flying. Children have little power and are acutely aware of the superior strength and knowledge of adults. They are also conscious of their own mistakes while attempting to learn new skills. It is not surprising that they enjoy playing the role of a powerful being who is brave, strong, and good, and who solves every problem without making mistakes. By pretending in this manner, children can overcome some of their own feelings of fear, powerlessness, or incompetence.

Sometimes the favorite characters have evil powers, and the child pretends to kill and destroy rather than rescue others in distress. This kind of play can be a way of conquering fears. Taking on the role of a frightening monster may be the child's way of providing himself with therapeutic laughter about the very things that frighten him the most (as described in Chapter 2).

Superhero play can also help children explore concepts of good and evil. The characters are either all good or all bad, and this simplification helps children isolate the significant values that our culture endorses or rejects. Real people are always a mixture of good and bad traits, but often for reasons too complex for children to understand.

What about play that appears to be senseless and foolish?

Sometimes children act in silly ways that appear to have no purpose. Parents often find this kind of behavior irritating. In the follow example, a mother described her feelings about her four-year-old daughter's silly behavior.

> It's usually right around bedtime when she becomes humorous and silly, and does all these creative things like putting her pajamas on her head or her slippers on her nose. I tend to think of that as being out of control, and I give her lots of messages that it's time to be serious and to stop playing around and get ready for bed. I hear myself saying all these things, and I wish I could stop. It's hard for me to be fun-loving and playful with her.

Like the mother in this example, you may find it hard to tolerate this kind of behavior. Perhaps you feel that it's a waste of time. But this kind of play (which I call nonsense play) can actually be therapeutic for your child, especially if she laughs. Young children must learn hundreds of household rules and appropriate behaviors, such as how to get dressed, speak properly, brush their teeth, and eat with silverware. They must learn that it's not okay to interrupt people, take toys from other children, draw on the walls, or talk with their mouths full. The list is endless, and children cannot master all of these rules at once. They know that their behavior does not always meet their parents' approval, even when the parents are loving and non-punitive. This is why the freedom to playfully make mistakes and purposely do things wrong can feel very liberating. While acting silly in these ways, children can release painful feelings of inadequacy, frustration, anxiety, or powerlessness through therapeutic laughter. They are playing with the stress resulting from people's expectations for them to follow the rules.

Nonsense play can also help children overcome the frustrations that occur while learning new skills, even when there is no pressure from parental expectations. After struggling to master a skill, children naturally feel proud of themselves, but they may still have some residual frustrations that need to be released. This is why children often use nonsense play after accomplishing something new. A child who has recently learned to play a lotto game may match all the cards incorrectly while laughing. A child who has memorized a nursery rhyme may find it humorous to recite it incorrectly. Children who can change the rules in a situation where they have total control are creating a therapeutic situation for themselves. To young children, nonsense play is not only funny, it is therapeutic.

Try to be patient with your child's nonsense play, even when it occurs at inconvenient times. Your child will probably love it if you take a few minutes to act silly and laugh with her. Your participation will strengthen your emotional connection with each other. Furthermore, you may find that she is more cooperative after these joint sessions of nonsense play.

What kinds of toys are best?

The best toys for young children are those that inspire them to imagine, build, create, move, and think. To encourage thinking and other cognitive skills, a stimulating environment should include puzzles, containers of different sizes (for water or sand play), matching games, memory games, counting games, and objects to sort (based on color, size, or shape). As mentioned earlier in this chapter, card games and board games can further stimulate memory, math, and logical thinking skills. Children also benefit from playing with musical and rhythm instruments. A set of sturdy wooden blocks of different sizes and shapes is probably one of the best educational investments you could make.

To encourage fantasy play, give your child dolls, a doll house, small figures, puppets, toy cars, toy dishes, small animals, dress-up clothes, and a doctor kit. Craft materials are also important, specifically clay, crayons, and paint (including finger paint). With these materials, children can engage in the kind of symbolic play that is important for their emotional and intellectual development. To encourage creativity and innovation as your child grows older, you can provide him with additional craft supplies such as cardboard, scraps of wood and cloth, used thread spools, rubber bands, pipe cleaners, string, glue, tape, and a pair of scissors. He may amaze you with his constructions or inventions. As mentioned in Chapter 3, you can minimize the effect of gender stereotypes if you give similar toys to children of both sexes.

Some parents wonder whether they should give their children realistic-looking toys that resemble real objects, such as dolls with detailed facial features and realistic looking toy houses or barns. Or is it better to stay with unstructured, open-ended toys, such as a set of blocks and scraps of cloth, and let the children use their imagination to create their own fantasy scenes? There is no evidence that realistic-looking toys damage children's imagination. In fact, for very young children (under four years of age), realistic toys actually stimulate more fantasy play than less realistic ones. Perhaps this is because the symbolizing ability of very young children is still developing. As children become older, they can gradually dispense with realistic props and rely more on their own imagination. A good guideline for young children, however, is to avoid automated toys that can move by themselves or electronic toys that do everything with the press of a button. Children will benefit more from producing their own movements.

You can let your child guide you in your choice of toys. Children's need for fantasy is so strong that they are not likely to allow the presence of unnecessary props to interfere, as the following example of my daughter illustrates.

> One day at three years of age, Sarah was pretending to go on a hike and a picnic. She carefully filled an imaginary backpack with invisible provisions and food. Thinking she would enjoy using a real, child-sized backpack in her play, I offered her one that I had in the closet. Upon seeing it, she became angry, stamped her feet, and said very forcefully, "I don't need a backpack. I have a *pretend* backpack." Realizing her great need to fantasize, I returned the real backpack to the closet. I had learned a lesson!

Children also benefit from using real tools. Look for a child-sized broom, mop, hammer, and screwdriver (not plastic toys, but tools that really work). With this equipment (and under appropriate supervision), children can participate in real work around the home. Your child will naturally want to help and imitate you, so you can encourage this tendency as soon as it appears. Young children do not distinguish work from play.

Most children also enjoy other kinds of objects from the adult world. If you give your child old credit cards, catalogs, and empty food containers, he will probably incorporate them into his play. These objects are like magic windows that allow children to gain access to a small part of the mysterious and complex adult world.

Should I let my child play with guns and other war toys?

Some parents find war play offensive and do not let their children play with guns, while others feel there is no harm in such play. Even if you don't let your child play with guns, he may make his own out of sticks or cardboard, or simply use his fingers. You may find it difficult to watch your child engaging in such violent forms of play, as the mother of a five-year-old boy told me in the following example.

I don't have guns for him, but he'll use his hand or a stick. When he's over at his friend's house, they have cap guns that they carry around constantly. I don't like guns, and I've explained this to him. So now, any time that he talks about guns, he'll say, "You don't like them, do you Mom, but I do!" My husband says that he played with guns when he was little, and he's not a violent person. In fact he is a pacifist and a conscientious objector. He doesn't see any harm in gun play. I guess there's no harm in it, but I just get upset with all the toys in stores. I think it's awful. All those violent, horrible monsters and war toys! I hate it!

Chapter 3 explains why young children should be protected from witnessing violence, both in real life and in the media. However, this shielding is hard to accomplish, and most young children learn about wars, murders, and mass shootings through real life and books, as well as through news and entertainment media. This exposure to violence creates a need for children to understand and assimilate the information and to process their emotions of fear and confusion. Children can accomplish this assimilation and emotional processing through their war play. Contrary to what some parents fear, there is no evidence that children's self-initiated war play makes them more violent later on. Many pacifists admit to having played with toy guns as children.

As explained earlier in this chapter, children re-enact in their fantasy play everything they learn in an effort to assimilate the information. It is not surprising that children will want to play pretend killing games as soon as they learn about this kind of violence. Gun play indicates that the child is attempting to understand and assimilate information about killing: What is it? How does it work? Why would a person kill another person? How would it feel to kill or be killed? What are all the different ways a person can be killed?

Boys are more likely than girls to show an interest in weapons. These sex differences may be partly biological, but there is also a strong cultural influence. Many parents encourage their sons' interest in weapons by giving them toy guns, swords, or bows and arrows. Little boys also learn to associate weapons with men through the media. Little girls, on the other hand, learn that women are not usually involved in wars or other forms of violence.

Instead of banning your child's war play, you can help him deal with his fear and confusion about violence by encouraging laughter, as described in Chapter 2. If he points a finger at you and says "bang, bang, you're dead," a helpful response is to pretend to die as dramatically as possible. In this power-reversal game, you are letting him feel powerful while you play the part of a weak and frightened victim. If you play your role effectively, he will laugh and want to repeat the activity. You will not teach him to be violent. On the contrary, you will help him conquer his fear of death and violence through the tension release mechanism of laughter.

Children also use gun play to process their feelings of anger and frustration. If your child feels jealous and angry because of a new sibling, he can release some of this anger by symbolically killing a doll or stuffed animal that represents the baby. If he feels angry at you, he can express that feeling by pretending to kill you. The laughter in these situations is therapeutic. The more your child laughs, the quicker his anger will dissipate. You can help by acknowledging and accepting your child's feelings and by encouraging laughter.

Even though children can benefit from this kind of interactive play with the theme of violence, there is no need to support the war toy industry by buying war toys. Toy companies make huge profits by taking advantage of children's fears and their compelling need to understand violence. Children are quite capable of creating their own weapons with paper, cardboard, or other objects in the home. When you give your child a commercially made, realistic-looking toy gun, he may feel that you condone guns and killing.

Accepting your child's spontaneous war play is quite different. Your child knows that his own, home-made facsimiles are not the real thing and that the weapons come from his own imagination. Because of this, he can easily switch to other forms of play when he has had enough war play. For example, he can turn his home-made sword into a magic wand. Commercial war toys are too well-defined to allow for such flexibility. A plastic toy gun is nothing but a gun.

Another danger of realistic toy guns is that children may not be able to distinguish them from real guns. If children have access to real guns in their homes, they may play with them and pull the trigger, thinking that they are toys. If you have real guns in your home, you should keep them securely locked up and out of sight at all times.

In spite of your efforts to restrict commercial war toys, your child may receive them as gifts from others or may decide to spend his own money on them. It is not easy to keep these items out of your home. When my son began to receive war toys as birthday presents from his friends, I felt very uncomfortable with these toys, but I decided that the most respectful approach was to let him decide which toys he wanted to own. The following example describes how his war play evolved over the years.

> When Nicky was five years old, he first heard about wars. He soon began to make guns, swords, and bombs out of paper and cardboard, and try them out on various members of the family. His friends at school introduced him to popular, small war-like figures when he was about six years old, and it wasn't long before he began collecting them himself. He received them as birthday presents from his friends and spent his own money on them. He soon had quite a collection of both "good guys" and "bad guys," representing two teams at war against each other. He and his friends would spend hours at a time playing with the figures, enacting all sorts of war scenes, which became more complex as they grew older. Then one day, when he was eight years old, the entire living room was the location of an elaborate set-up with his figures and other equipment. An unusual scene attracted my attention: all of his figures were sitting together in a circle, both the "good guys" and

the "bad guys." I asked him what was going on, and he replied, "They've decided to join forces, so they now share one big fort, and they're having a conference." Apparently, evil forces were still lurking somewhere in the universe, but at least the two opposing armies on earth had overcome their animosity! If I had forbidden my son's war play, would he ever have had the opportunity to work out the details of a peace conference?

How can I be a helpful participant in my child's play?

Don't underestimate the importance of joining your child in playful activities. By playing with her in specific ways, you can strengthen your connection, help her work through fear and trauma, and also resolve behavior problems. I call these specific kinds of play *attachment play*. Some of these activities are described in previous sections of this book. This section summarizes these and includes a few more. (See my book, *Attachment Play*, for more information.)

One of the most helpful ways to play with your child is called nondirective, child-centered play. Provide materials for fantasy play and then let your child decide what to do while you give her your full attention. This activity will allow her to feel loved and accepted. You don't have to do much other than watch, listen, and respond to your child. If she requests more active involvement from you, she will feel supported if you willingly enter into her fantasy world and do whatever she wants. For example, she may ask you to buy food at her pretend store or take the role of the mommy in a doll scene. To distinguish these focused play times from other kinds of play, you may want to refer to them as "special time" or "Mommy (Daddy) time."

Researchers have found that nondirective, child-centered play has surprising benefits. As little as half an hour, once a week of this activity can reduce behavior problems in children and increase their willingness to cooperate. This activity creates a healthy balance for children. Most of the time, we adults expect them to accommodate to our world and obey our rules. When, for a change, we enter into their fantasy world and become an obedient playmate who participates within the structure created by them, they have a chance to be in control, create their own rules, and develop a feeling of powerfulness and mastery. Playing with other children does not have the same benefits as playing with a parent.

Two kinds of parent/child play were mentioned earlier in this chapter. You can encourage symbolic play if your child has experienced a traumatic event, and do some silly nonsense play together to strengthen your connection with your child. Another beneficial activity, called contingency play, is to obey your child's commands or imitate her. This will allow her to feel powerful and in control. A good imitation game is follow the leader, in which you imitate everything your child does.

Separation games such as hide and seek can be therapeutic, especially if your child has been separated from you. Be aware that your anger or impatience can feel like a physical separation to your child and result in separation anxiety. Luckily there are ways to repair your connection. The act of hiding creates a non-threatening separation between you and your child. When you find each other, the joyful reunion brings reassurance, and your child learns that she can survive short separations from you. In addition, any laughter during the game will help her release anxiety. So if your child hides and wants you to find her, don't hesitate to participate in the game. This activity will allow her to feel safe and re-connected to you.

Another helpful way to play with your child is to pretend to be fearful, incompetent, or powerless, as described in the section on gun play. This power-reversal play doesn't always need to involve war play. If your child pretends to be a lion, play your part by pretending to be frightened and running away, but then be sure to let your child catch you. The primary goal is laughter, which dissolves anger and fear, and helps strengthen your bond with your child.

Regression games are activities in which your child pretends to be a baby. Many young children love to act younger than they are, especially if they have a younger sibling. Don't be afraid to encourage this kind of play and to rock your child like a baby, sing a lullaby, feed her from a bottle, or put imaginary diapers on her. She will act more grown up when she is ready to do so. Finally, two additional kinds of helpful play include any enjoyable activity with body contact (such as a hand-stacking game) and cooperative games in which nobody wins or loses.

You can increase the effectiveness of your parent/child play-times by following a few basic guidelines. Try to remain flexible while avoiding the temptation to direct the activity or turn it into a teaching situation. Find ways to laugh *with* your child, but not *at* her, and avoid tickling or teasing your child. There is no need to interpret or analyze your child's play, although you may wish to do this privately. A final guideline is to avoid using play to distract your child from crying. When your child cries, the most helpful approach is to accept the tears and listen with empathy, as described in Chapter 1.

Recommended forms of parent/child play (attachment play)

- Nondirective, child-centered play

- Symbolic play with specific props or themes

- Contingency play (including imitation games)

- Nonsense play

- Separation games

- Power-reversal games

- Regression games

- Activities with body contact

- Cooperative games and activities

What if I become bored while playing with my child?

Many parents recognize the importance of playing with their children but become bored or impatient while doing so. The mother of a four-year-old expressed these feelings in the following example.

> Her school schedule is Mondays, Wednesdays and Fridays, and I always think that on Tuesdays and Thursdays we'll have the whole day together. Well, it ends up that I usually want to do other things like clean up my desk and order something from the Internet that I have been putting off doing for months. I'm not organized enough to get these things done when she's at school. When she says, "Mommy, play with me," I sit down to play with her, but then I get frustrated. I don't have the patience to play games her way, and I begin to wonder why I didn't invite some other child over to play with her! The quality time together that we dream of just doesn't happen that much.

Why is it so difficult for us to give children the amount and quality of attention that they seem to need? Several reasons probably account for this difficulty. We adults don't always find our children's play very stimulating because we have already learned the things they are practicing. Furthermore, playing with a child involves a tremendous amount of relaxed attention. You may feel overwhelmed with so many other things to do that you have little time or attention left for your child. Or perhaps your own parents never played with you, so you have no role models for that kind of interaction. Maybe you still yearn for that kind of attention. This unmet need can contribute to the reluctance you may feel about playing with your own child. You may find it helpful to explore your childhood memories related to play.

Some parents find play sessions more tolerable when they set a timer for ten to twenty minutes and let their child know that they are available until it rings. On days when you just can't muster the energy or motivation to play with your child, you can pursue your own hobbies, interests, or housework while letting your child participate in some way. For your own well-being, as well as that of your child, it is important to create a balance between adult-centered activities and child-centered ones. Without this balance, you may begin to resent your child. The amount of time you spend on your own work and interests at home will obviously depend on your child's age, individual needs, and personality.

Be sure to attend to your own needs for rest, work, exercise, time alone, and time with other adults. Most parents feel the need for some time away from their children, and they find that they have more attention for their children when they are not constantly with them. Finding other people to care for your child is one way to create this balance. If you are a full-time parent, but want or need an outside job, your relationship with your child will probably be better if you find a job. If you stay home with your child full time out of sense of duty, your child could begin to feel anxious or insecure because of your frustration and resentment.

Once you have achieved a balance in your own life and taken care of your own needs, you will have better attention for your child during the times when you are together. Also, expressing your boredom and frustration (with another adult, away from your child) may help to dissipate some of these feelings and allow you to have better attention for your child. The more you play with your child, the easier and more enjoyable it will probably become.

In the following example, a mother reported to me how pleasurable it was when she decided to focus her attention on her three-year-old daughter, even though this was sometimes difficult for her to do.

I've noticed that when I really decide to give her attention, it's always a delightful experience. She'll paint and sing at the same time about all the colors she's using. It's just amazing. I love watching her. When I let her play the way she wants to, it helps me to reclaim my own past childhood memories and creativity.

How can I minimize the importance of winning, and what about children who cheat?

Most Western cultures place a large emphasis on competition. In these cultures, it is difficult to find a game for children in which nobody wins or loses. Many people automatically think of all games as contests and cannot imagine having fun without trying to beat someone else. Competitiveness also permeates our educational system to such an extent that it becomes difficult to envision a non-competitive learning environment.

A strong emphasis on competition has several disadvantages. Researchers have found that people of all ages learn and perform much better in cooperative rather than competitive settings. Furthermore, playing a cooperative game (in which nobody wins or loses) activates a different part of the brain than playing a competitive one. The part of the brain activated during cooperative play (the orbitofrontal cortex) is the location where decision making and impulse control occur, such as the control of aggressive behavior.

Studies have found that active cooperative group games with aggressive children between the ages of three and five years helped reduce aggressive behavior and increase cooperation with their peers. Other studies found that providing cooperative learning experiences for older children produced similar results.

Children do not normally have the concepts of winning or losing until we teach these to them. In fact, most young children enjoy cooperative games just as much as competitive ones. During free play, children's ability for successful peer cooperation increases after the age of two, and children who have more experience playing with other children tend to cooperate more effectively. It's possible that this ability to cooperate is also partly genetic and has evolved in human beings because of its survival value.

The culture in which children live can influence their tendency to cooperate. When researchers gave children a choice between playing a game cooperatively or competitively, the researchers found that the choice to compete increases after the age of five, but only for children who live in highly competitive cultures such as the U.S.

If you wish to create a non-competitive home environment, a first step is to use a non-authoritarian approach to discipline. The use of punishments or rewards inevitably creates an atmosphere of competition and a feeling in children of winning or losing conflicts. You can also discourage contests and avoid comparing your children to each other. If you propose a race to see who can be ready for bed first, you are setting up a situation in which one person will win and the others will lose. If you want to motivate your children to hurry while discouraging competition, you can suggest, "Let's set the timer for ten minutes and see if we can *all* be ready for bed before it rings."

Playing cooperative games can also help. Look for games and sports in which nobody wins or loses, or invent cooperative versions of traditional ones. You can also foster cooperation by engaging your child in family activities such as making music or cooking together.

How to minimize competition at home

• Avoid the use of punishments and rewards.

• Avoid comparing your children to each other.

• Avoid contests to motivate your children.

• Play cooperative games and sports.

• Do cooperative activities (music, cooking, etc.).

When children acquire the concept of winning, it can become associated with their sense of self-worth, but this is more likely to occur in children who already have low self-esteem. Children who feel loved, secure, and confident are less likely to become upset when they lose a game. In fact, they may even congratulate their opponent and comment about how well she played. Such children can enjoy the challenges of competitive games without attaching too much importance to the outcome. Children who have low self-esteem may feel so anxious about the possibility of losing a game that they resort to cheating. It is so important to them to win the game that they break the game rules, even though they risk being "caught" and criticized.

I think of cheating behavior as a plea for help with feelings of anxiety and insecurity. If your child begins to cheat while playing a game with you, you will probably not find it very effective to correct or criticize her, or to explain the virtues of following the rules. This approach will not motivate your child to improve her game strategy or her honesty. Instead, you can use the opportunity for some therapeutic play. You will need to abandon the idea of following the game rules and playing the game seriously. Instead, turn the activity into a power-reversal game in which you pretend to be very upset at the fact that you are losing. The goal is to encourage your child to laugh, which will help her release feelings of anxiety. The following example illustrates how I turned a cheating situation into a power-reversal game with therapeutic laughter.

> I was playing a game of checkers with a six-year-old boy, but every time I was about to capture some of his checkers, he claimed that the rules did not allow me to do that. He also created kings for himself when he thought I wasn't looking. When he kept changing the rules, I did not argue, but let him do what he wanted. I also exaggerated the difficulties I was experiencing, saying, "This is a difficult game. I don't think I'm going to win." He began to giggle. Whenever a new king appeared on the board, I said with mock surprise, "What? Another king! Where did that come from? How did you do that?" He laughed heartily and began cheating more openly. I kept him laughing throughout the entire game and let him win.

When you transform a cheating situation into a therapeutic power-reversal game, you will not be encouraging your child to become even more dishonest. On the contrary, she will use the opportunity to release anxiety through laughter, and she will probably be *less* likely to cheat in the future.

Even children who feel confident and secure occasionally enjoy changing game rules. Very young children who are just learning the concept of rules may want to experiment with changing the rules in their favor. But this behavior is different from the kind of cheating that older children do. The most helpful approach, regardless of your child's age, is to encourage laughter and forget about playing the game seriously.

Not all rule changes are a form of cheating. Some children enjoy creating their own game variations. Inventing games is a form of creativity that involves logical thinking and strategic planning. If you play the games that your child invents, you will encourage her creative thinking abilities. Furthermore, you may find her games more enjoyable than store-bought ones!

Exercises

Explore your childhood

1. Did you have enough time and space to play as a child? Did you have enough toys (or too many toys)? What was your favorite toy or game?

2. Do you remember playing alone as a child? Playing with a sibling? Playing with your parents? Did your parents play with you as much as you wanted?

3. Recall one or two of the most enjoyable play experiences you had as a child (alone or with someone else).

Express your feelings about your child

1. How do you feel about the way your child plays? Do you wish your child would play with different toys or be less noisy, messy, bossy, or silly?

2. Spend half an hour paying attention to your child and doing what your child wants to do (nondirective, child centered play). How did you feel? Did you become bored? Did you feel an urge to teach or direct your child's activities?

3. Does your child ever cheat or want to change the rules of a game? How does that make you feel?

Nurture yourself

1. Buy yourself a toy or game, perhaps something you wanted as a child but didn't have.

2. Find ways to bring more play, joy, and laughter into your life, with or without your children (for example, attend a costume party, visit an amusement park, watch a funny movie).

Chapter 5

Conflicts and Challenges

ONE OF THE MOST difficult parenting tasks is to change children's unwanted behavior without damaging their self-esteem or the parent/child connection. This chapter describes the disadvantages of an authoritarian approach, the underlying causes of behavior problems, and ways to change children's behavior without using punishments or rewards. Sibling rivalry and problems with other children are discussed in Chapter 6.

What are the effects of punishment?

Punishment is something hurtful or disagreeable done to a child in an effort to change his behavior. Corporal punishment includes hitting, spanking, slapping, beating, or whipping. Non-corporal punishment includes deprivations such as withholding attention, freedom, food, or privileges. Non-corporal punishment also includes requiring a child to do extra chores.

After decades of research on spanking, the results are conclusive. Spanking does not make children more compliant, and it can cause lifelong emotional problems. Studies have shown that the more children are spanked, the more likely they are to defy their parents, become aggressive, and suffer from emotional problems and cognitive difficulties. Adolescents and adults who were spanked as children are more likely to exhibit anti-social behavior and suffer from anxiety, depression, and substance abuse.

A major risk of instilling blind obedience to authority with the use of corporal punishment is that the child may grow into an adult who will blindly obey all authority figures. He may lose the ability to think for himself and make wise decisions. In her book, *For Your Own Good*, Alice Miller analyzed the childhoods of the Nazi leaders and concluded, "Among all the leading figures of the Third Reich, I have not been able to find a single one who did not have a strict and rigid upbringing." To the end of their lives, these people carried out every single command given to them, without hesitating or questioning.

Do other forms of punishment cause less damage? The use of time-out is a popular nonviolent form of punishment, but this approach has several hidden pitfalls. First of all, there is the problem of enforcing a time-out. There must be an underlying threat of a worse consequence (perhaps more deprivations or a spanking) if the child does not obey, because most children will refuse to isolate themselves unless they fear a worse punishment.

Another pitfall of time-out is that withdrawal of love and attention can cause children to feel anxious, confused, unloved, and insecure. Children need to know that their parents love them unconditionally. Even though you make a distinction in your own mind between your child and his behavior, your child cannot make this same distinction. To him, the forced isolation implies that you don't love him and don't want to be with him.

Another drawback of time-out and all other forms of punishment is that these approaches do not address the underlying reason for the child's behavior, nor do they teach children useful conflict-resolution skills. Punitive consequences do not inspire children to think productively about what they did wrong. On the contrary, punishments breed resentment and anger, which can turn into open rebellion as children grow older.

Finally, all forms of punishment can damage your relationship with your child. When you demand blind obedience with the threat of a punitive consequence, your child will inevitably feel misunderstood, unloved, powerless, and perhaps even unsafe. He will look elsewhere for the unconditional love and understanding that he needs and deserves.

Most parents who use punishment do so with good intentions

and do not know how else to cope with their children's difficult behavior. A common belief is that children need some kind of painful consequences when they act inappropriately so they will learn to change their behavior. This is a mistaken notion, yet it seems to be ingrained in our culture. Children do not need painful consequences, but they do need connection, understanding, information, and loving limits. Fortunately, it's possible to change children's behavior and set limits without the use of any kind of punishment.

What about rewards?

As punishment has become less popular, many parents use rewards or bribes to change their children's behavior. The use of rewards does not harm children in the same way that punishment does. Unfortunately, however, rewards have several drawbacks, which are similar to those associated with the use of praise (as explained in Chapter 3).

Rewards are actually quite similar to punishments. Once you set up a reward system for your child, she will feel punished when she fails to earn a reward. She may also feel resentful and angry about being controlled in this way.

Rewards can also be deceptive. When you use rewards, you have no guarantee that your child is learning any meaningful values. She may put her toys away to obtain the reward you promised, but will she do this because of respect for order or for the feelings of others? Most likely, the only motivating factor will be the desire for your reward. So the use of rewards actually teaches children to think only about themselves and to strive for immediate gratification. Are those the values that you want your child to acquire? What will happen when a drug dealer offers your child something more enticing than your gold stars?

Another drawback is that the use of rewards, like the use of punishment, does not address the underlying reason for children's behavior and does not teach children useful conflict resolution skills. For example, if your child's anxiety leads to bedtime problems, no reward will help her feel less anxious.

Reward systems can become complicated. You may be faced with the difficult situation of deciding whether older children should receive more or fewer rewards than younger ones, which behaviors should be rewarded, and how long to keep giving the rewards. Children are quick to point out anything that they consider unfair, especially when they have siblings.

One of the major disadvantages of rewards is that they can backfire and have the opposite effect of what you want. An interesting experiment demonstrated that preschool children who received an expected reward after doing a drawing activity subsequently lost interest in the activity when the reward was removed. On the other hand, children who were never rewarded in the first place did not lose interest. It seems that when we reward children, they comply only to obtain the reward and lose touch with their original interests and their own intrinsic motivation.

Our job as parents is to give our children the strength and self-confidence to *resist* being manipulated by anything or anyone, including advertisements, drug dealers, peers, and authority figures, no matter how alluring the rewards are. We need to teach our children to think about the long-term consequences of their behavior on others (not only the immediate personal consequences). The use of gold stars, candy, stickers, money, attention, or any other reward, innocent as it might seem, teaches children to become egocentric while letting others control their behavior and their lives. It encourages children to do things for the wrong reasons.

There are some situations in which young children enjoy receiving rewards for their accomplishments. In the scouting movement, children can earn merit badges for completing specific tasks, and children's libraries sometimes offer summer reading programs in which children can earn a prize for each book they read. As long as the children have freely *chosen* to put themselves into this kind of reward situation, they will probably experience it like a game, and it will not have all the negative consequences of rewards described in this section. The problems with rewards are more likely to occur when an authority figure imposes a reward system on children with the goal of controlling their behavior.

Behavioral psychologists have researched extensively the use of rewards and punishments, originally with rats and pigeons, but also with human beings. There is no doubt that it's possible to change children's behavior with this behavioral approach to discipline. But even though such a system may appear to work when your children are little, you may encounter problems when they reach adolescence, because you will run out of ways to control them. Also, they will become increasingly resentful of your attempts to do so and may even rebel against your authoritarian approach. Our role as parents is not to train our children like circus animals, but to treat them with respect and provide the kind of information and emotional support that will allow them to make good decisions about how to behave.

What causes children's behavior problems?

Children sometimes act in uncooperative, annoying, hurtful, destructive, or even dangerous ways. Parents naturally want to change these unacceptable behaviors, and it is possible to accomplish this goal without the use of either punishments or rewards. The key to this approach lies in understanding *why* children act the way they do. Three major reasons account for unacceptable behavior: the child has a legitimate need, lacks information, or is upset.

The child has a legitimate need

Unmet needs can cause difficult behavior. A hungry little boy, whose father is busy at the computer, may try to gain his father's attention by making noise or taking things from his father's desk. Young children cannot easily wait for food when they are hungry, and they cannot always verbalize their needs.

One of children's most basic needs is for connection, and those who feel disconnected from their parents will find ways to be noticed, perhaps by clinging, whining, or picking a fight with a sibling. If their behavior makes their parents pay attention to them, it will serve its purpose, even when the parents respond with anger. People sometimes say of a demanding child, "He's only trying to get attention," implying that he shouldn't be given any, because it's not a legitimate need. However, attention and connection are basic, legitimate needs.

Children also have a great need for stimulation, and boredom can lead to unacceptable behavior. They cannot be expected to wait patiently in restaurants or other public places with nothing to do. They also need to move their body and cannot sit quietly for long periods of time.

There are many other needs, of course, and our primary job as parents is to fill our children's needs to the best of our ability. This doesn't imply that we should give them whatever they want, because wants and needs are not necessarily the same. (My daughter wanted to have horses and live in a castle!) But we can try to discern their genuine needs in each situation.

The child lacks information

Conflicts and behavior problems often arise because children have insufficient information about the consequences of their behavior. They must learn that windows are breakable, people don't like crumbs in their beds, busy streets are dangerous, and thousands of other facts. One of our jobs as parents is to provide children with the information they need to live safely and happily in our society. It is interesting that the word "discipline" comes from a Latin word meaning to teach.

The child is upset or suffers from unhealed trauma

A third possible reason for unacceptable behavior is the child's emotional state. A child who is feeling sad, jealous, frightened, confused, or frustrated might hit or bite other children, kick the cat, become agitated and uncooperative, or behave in other obnoxious ways. Even when there is no current stress in his life, he could be struggling with painful emotions resulting from past unhealed trauma.

I had a client whose three-year-old son had been biting other children at his preschool for about three months. After some probing on my part to identify possible sources of stress or trauma, the mother realized that the boy's biting behavior had begun the same week that the parents first started talking about getting divorced.

They hadn't said anything to their son about it, but he must have felt that something confusing and terrifying was happening.

As I mentioned in Chapter 1, children experience hurts, frights, and frustrations on a daily basis, even with the most loving parents. When children have no healthy outlet for these emotions, they can become aggressive or destructive. No amount of punishment, teaching, or distraction will cure the underlying cause for this kind of behavior. Instead, these children need loving support so they can release their painful emotions through crying, tantrums, therapeutic play, and laughter.

Three reasons for behavior problems

• The child has a legitimate need.

• The child lacks information.

• The child is upset or suffers from unhealed trauma.

These three reasons account for most difficult behaviors. We need to discard the mistaken notion that children "misbehave" because of some inborn character trait. Children are not bad. They are little human beings with needs and feelings, and they are doing the best they can. When we create favorable conditions, they will become loving and cooperative.

How can I prevent behavior problems?

Prevention plays an important role in a non-punitive approach to discipline. It's possible to prevent many behavior problems and minimize conflicts in your family. First of all, you can try to meet your child's basic needs as accurately and promptly as possible. To help your child feel connected, you can set aside a half hour each day (or at least once a week) for nondirective, child-centered play (as described in Chapter 4). This one-on-one attention from you will reduce obnoxious or demanding behavior caused by an unmet need for attention. To meet your child's need for stimulation, you can provide toys and activities for times and places of potential boredom, such as a long car drive.

Another preventive step is to change your child's environment, which is sometimes easier than trying to change your child. Be sure to install child-proof locks and put fragile or dangerous objects out of reach. Rearranging your furniture could help to prevent some conflicts. For example, your child may be less likely to watch television if the TV set is in a back bedroom instead of the living room. You can also make changes to encourage your child's self-sufficiency. Your child will be more likely to hang up her own jacket (instead of dropping it on the floor) if you install closet hooks that she can reach easily.

Preparation and training can also help prevent behavior problems. If you are planning a dinner party, let your child know ahead of time what to expect and also what behavior you expect from her. You can plan activities for her to do on her own in case she becomes bored with the adult conversation. It is always helpful to rehearse new situations beforehand, especially potentially stressful ones, such as a visit to the dentist or a first day at school. You can use role-playing to give your child the information she needs, and nonsense play to help her release anxiety through laughter.

You can also prevent conflicts and increase cooperation by replacing authoritarian commands with choices. Your child will be more likely to cooperate if, instead of telling her to brush her teeth, you ask if she prefers to brush her teeth before or after her bedtime story. Limits are actually easier to enforce than commands, so feel free to set limits on what your child is allowed to do. Instead of telling your child to play in her room for an hour, tell her that you are going to be working at the computer in your own room for an hour, and request that she not bother you (assuming she is old enough to remain unsupervised for a while). She is then free to play in any room except yours, which will let her feel that she has some choices.

Perhaps the most important preventive step you can take is to allow your child to release painful feelings regularly through crying, play, and laughter. When children are free of pent-up emotions, they become more cooperative and less aggressive or disruptive.

Tips for preventing behavior problems

• Fill children's needs.

• Change the environment.

• Provide preparation and training.

• Give choices instead of commands.

• Allow children to release painful emotions.

What if my child and I have a conflict of needs?

In spite of your efforts to prevent behavior problems, your child will probably still act in inappropriate ways from time to time. When this occurs, the first thing to consider is whether or not he is experiencing an unmet need. Begin by looking at the situation from your child's point of view and ask yourself, "Does my child have a need that is not being met?" Once you have determined a need, try to fill it. Sometimes very little is required to fill a child's need, as the following example with my daughter illustrates.

When Sarah was three years old, she would often come to the dinner table without washing her hands, and she would refuse to do so when I asked her to. I could have withheld all food until she washed her hands or given her a penny each time she remembered to do so. But these solutions would have put me in the position of an authoritarian controller. Instead, I tried to put myself in her place. Often, she was very hungry and did not want to take the time to wash her hands. She found it difficult to postpone eating once she had seen all the food. Also, it seemed very important for her to have her own way and not submit to my authority. The solution I found was to tell her that she could have one tiny bite of food before washing her hands. This approach always worked. She would take one little bite and then go wash her hands without any further protests. Eventually, she remembered to wash her hands before eating.

The effectiveness of this approach resided in the fact that I transformed a confrontation of wills into a situation in which nobody lost the conflict. It allowed her to "save face." Even though I gave in to her wishes in a very small, almost symbolic way, it was sufficient to make her feel that I understood and was willing to meet her need.

When your own needs conflict with those of your child, you may find it more difficult to find a solution. The two traditional approaches for dealing with conflicts of needs are authoritarian and permissive. The authoritarian approach involves the use of rewards or punishments (or promises and threats) to compel the child to act in a way that allows the parent's needs to be met. The child loses the conflict and the parent wins. In the permissive approach, the parents give in and fill the child's needs at the expense of their own. The child wins and the parents lose. Neither of these situations is satisfactory. The children become resentful when the parents use an authoritarian approach, but when the parents are overly permissive, they often become resentful of the children.

It's usually possible to find solutions that meet everybody's needs. When the same conflict occurs frequently, it's best to wait for a time when it's not happening and when you and your child are feeling relaxed and connected. Begin by acknowledging your child's needs, and then explain your own. The most effective way to convey your needs is to use a communication technique called an "I-message." This term was first coined by Thomas Gordon in his important book, *Parent Effectiveness Training*.

An I-message has three components. Begin by describing the behavior that bothers you, then state your feelings, and then explain the impact on you in the context of your own needs. Here's an example: "When you take a long time to get dressed for school in the morning, I feel frustrated and worried because it makes me late for work."

The three components of an I-message

1. When you... (describe the child's behavior that bothers you)

2. I feel... (describe your feelings)

3. Because... (describe your unmet need or the impact on you)

After giving your child an I-message, invite him to help think of a solution that would satisfy both of you. Even very young children can contribute creative solutions for conflicts if we give them the opportunity to do so. In the example above, perhaps your child needs more time to prepare for school and would agree to let you wake him up 15 minutes earlier. If he needs more time to connect with you in the morning, you can suggest a ten-minute bedtime cuddle as part of the morning routine.

The following example illustrates how my first authoritarian attempt at solving a conflict-of-needs situation led to anger and aggression in my daughter. I then used an approach that worked.

When Sarah was six years old, she liked to get dressed on cold mornings in the bathroom with the electric heater on. However, she dawdled and wanted the heater to remain on for a long time. This aggravated me because I resented the waste (and cost) of electricity. I would go in after about five minutes and turn the heater off. This resulted in a scream-ing rage on her part because she hadn't finished getting dressed. No amount of explaining about the cost of elec-tricity seemed to help. She still dawdled. One time, she was so angry after I turned the heater off that she hit me. I realized that I was being authoritarian and disrespectful, and that there must be a better solution. One day (when we were not in the bathroom), I discussed the problem with

her. I used an I-message to clearly state my feelings and
needs, and then invited her to help think of a way to solve
our problem. She had no ideas to offer, so I suggested that
I could set a timer in the bathroom for five minutes and
leave the heater on until the timer rang. She liked the idea
of knowing exactly how much time she had but wanted to
negotiate about the length of time. Finally, we agreed on
five-and-a-half minutes! This solution worked beautifully.
She always dressed quickly from then on and never com-
plained when the timer rang and I turned the heater off.
In fact, she was often fully dressed *before* it rang and said,
"You can turn the heater off now."

An important aspect of this conflict-resolution approach is that
you discuss the problem with your child at a time when the conflict
is *not* actually happening. This distance from the actual conflict
allows both of you to feel more objective and less frustrated with
each other.

You can also do this kind of conflict resolution in the context
of a more structured process called a family meeting. Plan a regular time for the family to gather together, once a week, with the
goal of discussing conflicts. I recommend creating a written agenda
during the week, which consists of a sheet of paper (posted on the
refrigerator or some other visible place) where anybody can write
down a topic that they wish to discuss at the next family meeting.

At the meeting, discuss all the agenda items and encourage
everybody to use I-messages. For each conflict, invite all family
members to help find solutions. Children as young as four are
usually old enough to negotiate verbally and participate in the dis-
cussions, even though they may not be able to write on the agenda.

Be aware that family meetings are most effective for solving conflicts of needs rather than conflicts of values. If your child
refuses to eat broccoli, for example, that would be a conflict of
values, rather than a conflict of needs, because his behavior does
not interfere directly with your own needs. (See Chapter 7 for a
discussion of eating problems.)

Tips for family meetings

- Hold meetings once a week.

- Begin with appreciations.

- Have a written agenda (created during the week).

- Discuss conflicts of needs (rather than conflicts of values).

- Use I-messages and listen well to each other.

- Encourage everybody to suggest solutions.

- Strive for consensus.

How can I provide information to prevent behavior problems?

The second reason for unacceptable behavior is lack of information, as the following example of my son illustrates.

> One day, when Nicky was two years old, I was horrified to find him busily coloring the wall with his crayons. Although I was very upset, I realized that he simply didn't know any better. I explained to him that I wanted the wall to stay white, and I began scrubbing it clean. I invited him to help me clean it, and he did so quite willingly. It took us about an hour of hard work to clean it up. I then explained again that we color only on paper, not on walls, and I made sure that he always had a stack of paper. He never colored on the wall again.

I was careful not to make my son feel guilty about what he had done. I simply gave him the information he needed and let him see how much effort was required to clean the wall. I invited him to help me but did not force him to do so.

In this example, my son was old enough to understand the concept of a rule and to remember it. Children under two years of age do not yet have this ability. With a child that young, it's important to state your rule and to give information and explanations, but you cannot expect her to remember and follow your rule the next day. Instead of expecting your one-year-old child to learn household rules, you will need to baby-proof your home and supervise her closely. (See my book, *The Aware Baby*, for information about dealing with behavior problems in infants and toddlers.)

Even after your child can grasp the concept of a rule, you will not always obtain immediate results. You may need to repeat the rule many times and remind your child of the reasons for it. Try to be patient and think of yourself as a loving teacher or guide rather than a disciplinarian.

Another developmental milestone occurs around the age of seven or eight years, when children can more reliably understand another person's point of view. It's helpful to keep these developmental stages in mind in order to have realistic expectations about your child's behavior.

Stages of development for understanding information

- By 10 months: Children can understand simple commands.
  Ex: "Come here." "Don't touch! It's hot!"

- By 24 months: Children can learn simple household rules.
  Ex: "No drawing on the walls."

- By 7 or 8 years: Children can understand another person's point of view.
  Ex: "I can't see the TV when you're standing in front of it."

There are several ways to give your child information. Verbal explanations are obviously one way to explain the need for your rules and limits. Explain to your child that you don't want him to bring sand into the house because it could cause people to slip and fall. Sometimes a single word is sufficient. If you want to warn your child about a hot stove, you may find it more effective to point to the stove and say "hot!" instead of "don't touch."

Nonverbal demonstrations can be more effective than verbal explanations. To teach your child how to treat a cat, you can simply show her how to pet it. Young children learn quickly through imitation. Preparation for future events is another way to give information, as mentioned in a previous section. You can prepare your child verbally and also by role-playing situations ahead of time.

Another effective way to provide your child with information is to do nothing, but to let natural consequences occur. The following example illustrates the use of natural consequences with my daughter.

When Sarah was four years old, she took daily swim lessons for a few weeks. I became irritated by the fact that she never hung up her swimsuit and towel after we arrived home, but simply dropped them on the floor. I usually hung them up for her until I realized that it was her responsibility and that she was old enough to learn how to do so. I explained that her swimsuit would still be wet the following day if she did not hang it up. She had only one swimsuit and swim towel, so it was important for them to dry overnight. However, she did not seem to care, so I warned her that I would not hang them up for her, and she left them in a heap on the floor. The following day she was upset at having a wet swimsuit and towel. After her swim lesson that day, she asked me where and how to hang them up, and I showed her how to do it. After that day, she always hung up her swimsuit and towel, and I didn't need to remind her to do so.

It seemed that the only way for my daughter to acquire the necessary information in that situation was to let her experience the discomfort of using a wet swimsuit and towel. It is not necessary to shield your child from the consequences of her own actions if you feel that meaningful learning will occur. When you let natural consequences occur, your attitude is important. Try to remain objective and show empathy when your child experiences a disagreeable natural consequence, even though you might feel like saying, "I told you so."

Natural consequences can be inappropriate or even too dangerous in some situations. If your child continues to ride her tricycle into the street after you have explained the dangers, perhaps you can convey the necessary information by pointing out an animal on the road that has been hit by a car. If your child still does not obey your rule, you obviously cannot risk the natural consequence. Instead, you will need to enforce a rule that she cannot ride her tricycle unless an adult is with her. This is not punishment, although your child might protest or even cry.

How to give information to children
(when unwanted behavior results from lack of information)

- Verbal explanations

- Nonverbal demonstrations

- Preparation

- Natural consequences (but not artificial ones)

- I-messages

Natural consequences differ considerably from a discipline approach that some people call "logical consequences." These are artificially contrived penalties, and I do not recommend them. The logical consequence for a child who does not eat much at breakfast might be to withhold all food until lunch time, even if she becomes hungry. This artificial consequence is no different from punishment. It's an authoritarian approach that fails to respect the child. Why not simply let the child eat when she's hungry?

A final effective way to convey information is to let your child know the effects of her behavior on other people, including yourself. The use of I-messages is a useful way to convey this information, as described in the previous section.

How can I deal with behavior problems caused by stress or unhealed trauma?

Painful emotions such as fear, frustration, sadness, or jealousy can lead to a variety of behavior problems. If your child continues to act unacceptably after you have tried to meet all his needs and given all the necessary information, it's likely that he is feeling upset or is suffering from a past distressing event. The following chart lists some common behaviors that can be caused by stress or unhealed trauma.

Behaviors that can be caused by stress or unhealed trauma

- Hyperactivity, agitation

- Impulsiveness

- Aggression, violence, destructiveness

- Obnoxiousness, rudeness

- Stubbornness, refusal to cooperate

- Clinging, whining, demanding behavior

- Frequent crying or tantrums (attempts to heal)

Many parents wonder how to change these behaviors without resorting to the use of punishments or rewards. How can you respond to a child who hits other children, knocks down his sister's block tower, runs wildly around the house, refuses to cooperate, rudely demands another story, or flatly refuses to go to bed? Children who act in these ways are usually harboring painful pent-up emotions. The only approach that will bring lasting results is to help your child with his feelings by showing empathy and encouraging emotional release. When he feels safe to vent his emotions by crying, raging, or laughing, his painful feelings will dissipate and his behavior will improve.

To help your child feel safe enough to begin crying, he will need to feel connected to you, so begin by establishing a connection with him. Lower yourself to his level, make eye contact, speak kindly, and touch or hug him. This connection alone, however, may not be sufficient to stop his unruly behavior. Your child will probably also need a pretext to begin crying, which you can provide by setting a loving limit.

To set a limit, you can say kindly, but firmly, "We need to leave the playground now." Your limit may involve removing an object from your child's hand, for example a breakable toy that he is banging against the wall. Or you can limit what you are willing to do for him, for example, "I'm not going to read any more books to you tonight," or "I'm too tired to carry you, but I will hold your hand while we walk."

At other times, you may need to set a physical limit and use your strength (but not violence) to lovingly restrain your child's arms or legs if he is using them to hit or kick. You can say, "I'm not going to let you hurt anybody," and firmly hold both of his wrists. If necessary, pull him into your arms and contain his whole body in a loving embrace. A room can also serve as a safe place to keep him contained, but only if you stay with him. For example, take your agitated child to the bathroom and stay there with him for a while to prevent him from running wildly around the house. These limits are necessary restrictions that you place on your child's behavior. There is no need to use threats or punishment, or to harm your child in any way. Your goal is *not* to make your child feel bad or to show him who's the boss. On the contrary, you want him to feel safe, loved, and connected to you.

After you have set a loving limit, don't be surprised if your child begins to cry or rage. As explained in Chapter 1, tears and tantrums are natural stress-release mechanisms. Your child's crying is a good sign because it indicates a healthy release of the pent-up feelings that caused the inappropriate behavior. Your response to this outpouring of emotions is important. There is no need to give in and change the limit you have set, no matter how loudly your child protests. Your child will use the limit as a pretext to cry (the "broken cookie" phenomenon). So calmly maintain your limit, but stay with your child, reassure him of your love, acknowledge his emotions, and offer empathy. You can say, "I see that you really want me to read another story, but I am not going to do so right now. It's okay to be angry about that." There is no need to offer any further explanations.

If you are holding your child, he may struggle in your arms while raging and try to break free. Use your judgment about how long to hold him. Sometimes, your continued holding will allow him to fully release his painful emotions. His need to struggle could have its roots in prenatal trauma or a difficult birth. The message you are conveying is that he is safe with you and that the connection between you is stronger than his anger or terror. At other times, you may decide to release your embrace and see what he does. His behavior will indicate whether or not he has cried enough.

After your child has completed his outburst, he will probably become more relaxed, connected, and cooperative. The following example illustrates this approach with my son.

> One day at four years of age Nicky was acting very obnox-iously. He kept slapping the newspaper that his father was trying to read and then started slapping me. It seemed clear to me that he was asking for help with some painful feelings, so I brought him into the bedroom and held him in a warm embrace. He struggled a bit, but soon started

to cry. I held him and caressed his face lovingly while he screamed and cried hard. He kept asking for things, such as dinner, or to go to the bathroom. I told him gently that all those things could wait and that I was going to hold him for a while. He cried hard for about 15 minutes and then calmed down and almost fell asleep. Then he told me about a nightmare he had the previous night about thieves coming into the house. After that, he wanted to cuddle with me some more. He was delightful the rest of the day, with no trace of obnoxious behavior.

Another way to deal with disruptive behavior is to engage your child in specific kinds of play while encouraging laughter. This playful approach can be just as effective as the approach described above, and it is especially useful for children who do not cry easily, or for situations in which holding your child would not be possible or appropriate.

In the following example, a friend described her experience using a playful approach with a little boy she took care of regularly, and who was acting obnoxiously.

At Christmas we were away from one another for a week, and when we were back together, Jason (age two) seemed unhappy, but had stopped crying altogether. If I held him, he wouldn't cry. He was whiny and fussy, and he often angrily demanded things. However, the things he requested did not seem to satisfy him, and he sometimes tried to hit me. I sensed that he had a lot of pent-up distress, but he seemed too afraid to "let go" with me. His father had temporarily moved out, and Jason was probably feeling terrified. I decided to use a more playful approach and to encourage laughter. One day, we had been at a skating rink, and it was time to go, but Jason didn't want to leave. In the car, he said in a bratty and angry tone of voice, "I want to stay at the skating rink." I acted silly and mimicked him while making a very goofy face and showing as much acceptance as possible. I was trying to convey that his anger did not upset or unravel me, that there was plenty of room for it, and I wouldn't take it personally. Within a few seconds, he was laughing his head off and seemed more relaxed with me than he had been in weeks. The whining decreased, and he seemed much less angry. Each time he was angry, I would be light and playful and silly with him. The next day, we were outside in the snow, and he started to get very frustrated going up a hill. When he began to whine, I continued being silly and light, and then he began crying spontaneously, and so much came out! I got down at his level and gave him my attention. His sobbing sounded more like grieving than anger. I nearly cried with joy myself, because it seemed to free him so. It was the first time in over six weeks that he had cried. I was certain that he had really needed to, but that he just couldn't feel safe enough to do so. The difference in his mood immediately after crying was phenomenal. He became calm, natural, peaceful, and happy. All clinging and demandingness ceased. It was really something.

In this example, the woman's silly mimicking of the child allowed him to feel safe and to laugh, which probably cleared away some of his built-up tension. Later, he felt safe enough to cry, which helped him release deeper emotions. When you use a playful approach like this one, make sure that your child knows you are not teasing him.

Active power-reversal play is especially effective with children who are acting aggressively or violently. Engage your child in a pillow fight in which you pretend to be weak or clumsy. Play your part by falling dramatically to the ground. If he laughs during this activity, you are on the right track. The laughter indicates that he is releasing anger and frustration. I often recommend this approach to clients whose children are aggressive, and the positive change in their children's behavior after such pillow fights sometimes astounds them. (See Chapter 4 for more about therapeutic play and also my book, *Attachment Play*.)

Two ways to deal with aggressive
or disruptive behavior
(caused by stress or unhealed trauma)

Loving limits and crying
- Make a connection.
- Set a loving limit (on your child's behavior or on your own).
- Encourage crying and raging.

Play and laughter
- Make a connection.
- Engage the child in specific kinds of play.
- Encourage laughter.

I sometimes hurt my child in anger.
What can I do about this?

If you have lost your patience and hit your child, you will probably feel guilty afterwards, because this isn't the kind of parent you want to be. When this happens frequently, you may find it helpful to explore the reasons for your anger and loss of self-control. The same three reasons for unwanted behavior apply to you as well as your child: (1) you have an unmet need, (2) you lack information, or (3) you are feeling stressed or are suffering from unhealed trauma.

The first step is to take care of your own needs. You can't be the kind of parent you want to be when you have unmet needs. Are you getting enough sleep, exercise, and free time? Are you frustrated because you are a full-time parent but wish you had an outside job? Many parents are physically and emotionally exhausted much of the time. You are always justified in asking for the kind of help that would allow you to be a better parent.

The second possible reason for your impatience is lack of information about child development. Are your expectations too high for your child's age? Perhaps you worry about behavior that is actually quite typical. Be sure to inform yourself about normal stages of development. This information could help you better understand your child's behavior and become more tolerant of it.

The third reason is either current stress in your life or unhealed trauma from the past. Do you have health, relationship, or financial problems? If so, try to obtain the help and support you need. If you are struggling with unhealed childhood pain, you may find yourself frequently triggered by your child's behavior. When your child does something for which you were punished (for example a temper tantrum or a fight with a sibling), you may find it difficult to remain calm and objective. Your first impulse may be to punish your child in the same way that you yourself were punished. Some people are unaware of their own childhood trauma until they become parents. Some are even shocked at the intensity of their anger and wonder where it came from. If you suffered from abuse or neglect, your child's behavior will probably trigger you frequently.

If you often lose patience with your child and think that the root cause may be your own unhealed childhood pain, consider joining a support group, obtaining counseling or therapy, or asking a good friend to listen to you while you explore memories and express emotions. If you fear that you will seriously harm your child, don't hesitate to call a child abuse hotline. You can also leave the room, hit a pillow, or scream into a pillow. Some parents hold their breath and count to ten. This might calm your anger temporarily, but it is much healthier to let your feelings out rather than hold them in. Remember also to congratulate yourself for all the times when you did *not* hit your child, even though you felt a strong urge to do so. You deserve to feel proud of those moments of self-control.

When children develop emotional or behavioral problems, parents are often the first to be blamed. Yet our society does not offer parents the training or support they would need to do a better job. In spite of these difficulties, I firmly believe that it's possible to treat our own children better than the way we ourselves were treated. I am continually amazed at the inner resources and strength of the parents who consult with me and who are struggling to raise their children with love and patience, in spite of the parents' own past history of punishment, abuse, or neglect.

If you have struck your child in anger, hug her, tell her you love her, and apologize for your behavior. Let her know that she did not deserve to be hit and that she is a good person. Give her a chance to cry if she needs to, and don't be surprised if she says she hates you. In the following example, a mother described her experience of hitting her four-year-old daughter.

> One time I remember, I had just bought her some cards, and we were playing with them, but she started crunching them up. I was so shocked that I hit her hand. Well, she went into hysterics and cried very hard. Afterwards, we had a talk, and I explained to her (as the tears were coming down my face) that I should have used my words. She seemed to really understand that I had something to work on. I didn't know how to use my words, and using words is a lot better than hitting.

How can I get my child to help with household chores?

Children do not begin life with a distinction between work and play. They find everything fun, including those tasks that we think of as chores such as cooking, cleaning, and doing laundry. If you do not enjoy housework, you may find it difficult to convey a relaxed, fun attitude about it to your own child, and you may find yourself nagging him to help and threatening him if he does not.

Young children normally imitate what their parents do, including chores around the home. If you encourage this tendency at an early age, your child will be more likely to help with chores later on. At first, your two-year-old's attempts to set the table or sweep the floor will not be perfect, and chores may take longer to complete when you let your child help. But your patience will pay off in the long run.

Chores are more enjoyable when they provide moments of connection and cooperation. As your child grows older, he is more likely to continue helping if you do chores together. Instead of expecting your child to put his toys away by himself, offer to do it with him. Also, don't forget to provide the information and training that your child needs. Take the time to teach him how to organize his toys, set the table, sort the laundry, or feed the cat, if those are the jobs you want him to do.

Some parents try to motivate their children to do chores by paying them or rewarding them in other ways. But your goal is to build on your child's natural desire to contribute and cooperate simply because he feels part of the family. When you give rewards, you are teaching him to do the chores for his own personal gratification. Are those the values you really want him to learn? If you wish to give your child a weekly or monthly allowance to help him learn how to manage money, that's fine, but it's best to keep those payments separate from the issue of household chores.

Instead of using a reward system, try a playful approach. Set a timer and aim to beat the clock while doing a chore together, or put on a piece of music and try to complete a specific task before the music stops. Pretend to be good fairies secretly cleaning up the house to surprise Mommy when she comes home.

Children are usually more eager to help when they have a choice, so let your child decide which chores to do. You can do this in the context of weekly family meetings (when you also discuss conflicts). Give your child a list of chores and ask him to select the ones that he is willing to do during the following week. Don't be surprised if your child agrees to do a chore for a while, but then wants to switch to another one.

I never rewarded either of my children for doing chores, and I had no trouble motivating them. When my daughter was four years old, one of her chores was to mop the bathroom floor with her child-sized mop. She liked the fact that her small mop fit into the space behind the toilet and that the adult-sized mop did not. My children often grew tired of their chores and wanted different ones, so we discussed this issue frequently at our family meetings. To remind them of the chores they had chosen, I prepared a sheet for each of them with a list of their chores (usually only one per day). Before they could read, I drew pictures to represent the different jobs. They enjoyed placing a star on the checklist each day after completing their chore. This was not a reward system, but simply a method to help them keep track and feel a sense of accomplishment.

Tips for encouraging children to help with household chores

- Begin early and encourage your child's tendency to imitate.

- Do chores together.

- Provide information and training.

- Avoid payments and other rewards.

- Be playful and make the chores fun.

- Discuss chores at family meetings and give choices.

What can I do about bedtime and naptime problems?

Bedtime problems rank high on parents' list of difficulties. You can reduce your child's resistance to bedtime by addressing the two factors most likely to create problems: your child's need for connection and her need for emotional release. It's normal for young children to resist falling asleep alone, and most prefer the presence of another person. As mentioned in Chapter 2, a fear of being alone in the dark may have had survival value in prehistoric times and be wired into children's brains through the process of natural selection. In fact, the young of all land mammals sleep next to their mothers. There is nothing wrong with catering to this need if your child wants you to stay with her until she falls asleep.

In my book, *The Aware Baby*, I recommend co-sleeping as the best way to meet your baby's need for closeness at night. If you enjoy co-sleeping, there is no reason to stop until your child is ready. She will eventually be willing to sleep in her own room, but the age at which this shift occurs varies considerably from one child to another. Children who can share a room with a sibling are more likely to outgrow the need for co-sleeping with their parents sooner than children who must transition to sleeping alone. Even though your child may be willing to sleep in a separate room, she may still request your presence at bedtime for several more years. She may also occasionally return to your room in the middle of the night, especially if she has a nightmare or feels ill. Any stress in your child's life will increase her need for connection at night.

The following example describes bedtime experiences with my daughter.

> Sarah slept next to me in my bed from the day she was born. As she grew older, she slept on a small mattress next to the big mattress (on the floor), which my husband and I shared. At three-and-a-half years of age, she wanted to sleep in the same room as her brother (age eight). At first she came back to our room in the middle of every night, but eventually she stayed in her own bed all night long. When she was just four years old, I was suddenly hospitalized for an emergency appendectomy. When I returned from the hospital, she began coming back to our room each night. This lasted for several months before she began sleeping through the night in her own bed again. Then, when she was four-and-a-half years old, she started preschool and once again began coming to our bed each night. At five years of age she was delighted to have a room of her own and happily went to sleep in it. However, she still needed somebody to stay with her until she fell asleep, and she still sometimes came to our bed in the middle of the night. I always let her finish the night close to me.

The second factor to consider is the need for emotional release. Accumulated painful feelings can cause tensions that prevent your child from falling asleep. Most babies need to cry at bedtime (while being held) to release tensions from the day, and this emotional release before sleep continues for many children well into the early childhood years. Your child may find a pretext to begin crying (the "broken-cookie" phenomenon): her favorite pajamas are in the laundry or you bought the wrong kind of tooth paste. You will obviously want to meet your child's real needs, but some of the things children cry about are not real needs. If your child becomes very demanding at bedtime, and you suspect that she has pent-up emotions, it may be appropriate to set a loving limit and welcome the crying or tantrum that results from your limit.

Some children become hyperactive or extremely agitated at bedtime. This high activity level may indicate a need to cry, and a physical limit combined with loving connection can help to unleash your child's tears. As described earlier in this chapter, you can take your child to the bathroom and stay there with her. Or you can hold her lovingly to contain her frantic movements. If you do nothing, be prepared for the possibility that your child may create a pretext to cry, perhaps by provoking a sibling to hit her. After your child has had a good cry, she will probably become relaxed and fall asleep easily.

Another approach for providing connection while encouraging emotional release is to engage your child in playful activities that produce laughter (as described in Chapter 4). A few minutes of a power-reversal pillow fight can work wonders with a child who is agitated or aggressive at bedtime. If your child is acting silly, a few minutes of nonsense play can help her feel connected to you while releasing tensions through laughter.

These guidelines of connection and emotional release also apply to naptimes. Be aware, however, that resistance to sleep during the day may be due to the fact that your child has outgrown the need for naps or does not need one at that particular time. Individual sleep needs vary greatly and depend on hereditary factors, rates of growth, health, amount of sleep at night, and amount of exercise. Some two-year-olds no longer need a daytime nap, while other children still need a daily nap at six or seven years of age, especially if they are allowed to stay up late in the evening. You can ease your child's sleep schedule to fit in with your lifestyle and culture.

Exercises

Explore your childhood

1. Were you punished as a child? How? Try to recall a few incidents and think about how you felt. Were you ever rewarded for "good" behavior? How did it make you feel?

2. Were you expected to obey your parents' commands without questioning? If so, how did you feel about this?

3. What memories do you have about household chores and bedtime? Do you wish your parents had acted differently?

Express your feelings about your child

1. Make a list of your child's behaviors that bother you the most. How do you feel about each one? What do you feel like doing to your child at those times? (This is not necessarily what you *should* do!)

2. Try to determine the underlying reasons for your child's unwanted behaviors. Do you think that any of them indicate unhealed trauma? How do you feel about that, and how can you help your child?

3. Does your child help around the home as much as you would like?

Nurture yourself

1. Are your basic needs being filled (for food, rest, time alone, etc.)? If not, what can you do to meet your needs?

2. Connect with other parents and compare solutions for your child's behavior problems. Look for parents who share your non-punitive approach.

3. If you frequently lose patience with your child and hit or yell, find a support group or therapist who can help you work through your childhood trauma.

Chapter 6

Friends and Foes

THIS CHAPTER FOCUSES on children's relationships with other people. Learning how to get along with others is one of the tasks of early childhood. Families can provide an excellent opportunity for learning social skills, especially if there is more than one child. This chapter also covers children's relationships with friends and with stepparents, as well as the topic of sexual abuse.

How can I prepare my child for a new baby?

It is important to prepare your child for the birth of a sibling. Depending on his age, you can prepare him by reading books, showing pictures, role-playing with dolls, or simply talking about the coming event. Your child will probably have many questions, which I recommend answering simply and directly. His questions may lead to topics such as where the baby came from or how it started growing, and this may be a perfect time to introduce basic concepts of human sexuality and reproduction. Avoid giving him the impression that the baby will be a new playmate, because he may become disappointed after he discovers that the baby can't do much. Instead, tell him that the baby will be quite helpless and will need considerable care.

As the due date approaches, your child will probably want to know exactly what will happen. He may ask how and when the baby will come out, where the mother will be, where he will be, or who will take care of him. You may need to answer these questions several times, and perhaps even rehearse the event by role-playing.

Your child may have concerns based on misconceptions. Near the end of my pregnancy, my son (almost five years old) worried that the baby might come out while I was asleep. I reassured him that the contractions would definitely wake me up! There is always a great deal of uncertainty surrounding birth: the sex of the baby, the day and time of birth, the possibility of an emergency Cesarean, or a disabled infant. It is better to prepare your child for these possibilities rather than give him information that may prove to be false. Tell your child that there are some things nobody knows ahead of time.

Many parents enjoy having their children present at the birth of a sibling, and some hospitals now allow this, but you may prefer a home birth. If you plan to have your older child present at the birth, he will benefit from some basic information about the stages of labor, regardless of where the birth takes place. Explain everything that will happen as well as everything that *could* happen. Don't omit descriptions of bleeding and the placenta. He needs to know that his mother will not be available to respond to his needs, hold him, or perhaps even speak to him during labor and birth. He also needs to know that his mother may make strange sounds and be in unusual positions, but that this behavior does not imply that she is ill. Also let him know your expectations about his behavior during the birth process, and reassure him that he can change his mind at any time if he does not want to be present. I recommend having an adult available, in addition to the labor coach, whose sole job is to pay attention to your older child.

Another important consideration is to make sure that your child feels entirely comfortable with the non-nursing parent, because that parent will play an important role after the baby is born. You can take steps during the pregnancy to have both parents share caretaking responsibilities, such as putting your child to bed, if you are not already doing so. Also have your child spend time with any other adults who will be taking care of him after the birth.

With these preparations, the birth of a sibling can be a wonderful and meaningful experience for your child, both emotionally and intellectually. He can begin bonding with his baby brother or sister right from the start. My son was present at the birth of his sister, as described in the following paragraph.

Nicky was almost five years old when his sister, Sarah, was born. Throughout my pregnancy he asked many questions, and we borrowed books from the library that described the growth of a baby and the birth process. As my due date approached, he was present when my husband and I rehearsed the various stages of labor and breathing techniques. We informed him about the birth process and the various possible outcomes (including an emergency Cesarean.) We agreed on a signal for him to be quiet: I would raise my right index finger to indicate the beginning of a contraction. We rehearsed this signal until he knew it well. The birth was to take place in a hospital that allowed families to be present. My mother was prepared to be with Nicky and to keep him occupied if he got bored. The birth went smoothly. Nicky was very attentive, obeyed my signals perfectly, and did not act frightened by the sight of blood. He enjoyed talking with the doctor and asking questions. He was allowed to hold his baby sister before she was one hour old. Right from the start, he felt extremely attached to her, and he asked to hold her frequently. He wished she could sleep in his room. He showed great interest in her growth and development and felt responsible for her safety and well-being. I am convinced that his presence at her birth helped create this strong bond between them. Although he did experience strong jealousy at times, he never tried to harm her.

What can I do about my child's resentment of a new baby?

The birth of a sibling requires a difficult adjustment for a child. It is as if a man said to his wife, "Honey, I am going to have another wife join our family. I love you very much, and I will also love my new wife. I hope you will love her too. I will be spending a lot of time with her, especially at the beginning." Adapt this idea to you and your partner, and think about how you would feel!

Even if you have prepared your child for the new baby, she may still feel angry and resentful. She may show this anger by trying to harm you or the baby, by becoming uncooperative or obnoxious, or by making unreasonable demands. She may also regress to infantile behavior, perhaps by refusing to feed or dress herself, requesting to nurse or use a bottle again, or wetting her pants well after becoming toilet trained.

Your child needs plenty of love and attention, and you can fill this need by setting aside some time each day for nondirective, child-centered play, even if only for ten or fifteen minutes (as described in Chapter 4). During this special time, try to devote your attention entirely to your child, and let her decide what to do. Depending on her age, she may want to play a game, cuddle, build with blocks, create imaginary scenarios with her toys, or pretend to be a baby.

Your child will probably also need to release feelings of resentment and anger, so be sure to accept her tears and tantrums (as described in Chapter 1). Don't be surprised if a small pretext triggers a major meltdown. The following example of my son illustrates intense raging triggered by jealousy of his baby sister.

> At five-and-a-half years of age, Nicky's jealousy of Sarah reached a peak, probably because his grandmother (who usually gave him lots of attention) was away for the summer. He became clingy and wanted to cuddle with me, especially when I was holding Sarah. One day, after I had spent an hour reading to him, he accidentally bumped his head and started crying. Just then, Sarah woke up. I picked her up and began to nurse her. This was just too much for Nicky, who screamed at the top of his voice, "I don't *want* you to hold Sarah!" He screamed and cried while trying to kick me. The crying was acceptable to me, but the kicking was not. No other adult was home to be with him, so I had no choice but to take the baby to another room and close

the door. Nicky cried loudly outside the door, but after a few seconds he promised not to kick me. So I opened the door and let him in. He sat next to us and continued to cry, but made no further attempt to kick me. After Sarah had finished nursing, he crawled into my lap and continued sobbing hard. Afterwards he was in a great mood and played quite happily by himself. He never showed this degree of jealousy again.

In this example, I did not enjoy forcing a separation between my son and me at a time when he needed connection, but it was only for a few seconds. Furthermore, my firm limit let him know that his kicking was totally unacceptable.

Power-reversal play can also be very helpful, because it allows children to use their aggressive energy in a harmless way and release tensions through laughter. In the following example, a mother described how she used playful wrestling to help her older child release anger toward his baby sister.

It started when Jimmy was over two years old and Nanda was five or six months old. He would start hitting me when I was nursing her, or else tear things apart, so that I could not sit and nurse her peacefully. He wanted my attention. It was very obvious. One day, when he was acting this way, as soon as I was able to give him attention, I wrestled with him and made it playful and fun. He would push against me with all his strength, and I would let him "win." He did lots of laughing. We did this for maybe half an hour. He loved it! Then he just relaxed and leaned on me and said, "Mommy, I love you." It was incredible! He's not usually that demonstrative about his love.

If your child tries to harm the baby, you will need to stop her immediately. The best way to accomplish this without making her feel rejected is to gather her into your arms in a loving embrace. Use gentle, but firm, restraint to prevent her from harming the baby. Your child will probably begin to cry and rage, and that will be a good thing. She may try to break free from your embrace, but this reaction does not imply that you are hurting her. On the contrary, your loving containment of her aggression gives her the opportunity to release tensions and anger (as described in Chapter 5). You can acknowledge her feelings and reassure her of your love, but also explain that you need to protect the baby. Try letting her go after a while to see what she does. If she tries to harm the baby again, you can hold her some more. After her rage has passed, she will probably become loving and gentle.

Some children express their jealousy verbally by saying "I hate you" or "I hate my baby brother." You may find it difficult to acknowledge and accept these statements, but if you can do so, your child will feel understood. A helpful response might be, "I understand how you feel. It must be very hard for you right now, with this baby around all the time. I bet you wish he would go right back where he came from, and then we could be together, just the two of us again, the way we used to be."

Another helpful approach is to engage your child in symbolic play. After the baby is born, you can give your older child a doll. Don't be surprised if she loves and cuddles it one day, but hits it or throws it on the floor the next day. If she tries to harm her baby sister or brother, encourage her to use the doll to show you what she feels like doing. You can also give her a doll family (or a teddy bear family) with the same number of adults and children as your real family. Observe how she plays with the doll family, or initiate a symbolic story using them as props. Begin by saying, for example, "Once upon a time there was a family with a little girl. One day, a new baby came to join the family. And then what happened?" Let your child continue the story.

The use of rewards or punishments can be deceptive. Such consequences might stop your child's overt aggression, but she will still feel angry and jealous, and these emotions could last a lifetime. Sadly, some adult siblings do not get along because they never had the opportunity to resolve their childhood jealousy. Another disadvantage of an authoritarian approach is that it could increase your child's resentment and feelings of disconnection. Furthermore, it may not even work. Your angry child may continue to harm the baby in devious ways when you are not looking. The only effective approach is to help your child with her feelings by providing opportunities for emotional release through tears, tantrums, play, or laughter.

Why do siblings fight with each other?

Several factors contribute to sibling rivalry. The more children there are in a family, the more likely they are to compete for parental attention. It is difficult for two parents to give adequate attention on a daily basis to more than two children. During prehistoric times, isolated nuclear families did not exist. Families probably lived in groups that included siblings, aunts, uncles, cousins, and grandparents, as is the case for more recent foraging societies. The children had many adults and other children to interact with and did not have to compete with their siblings for the attention of their biological parents. If you find it difficult to meet your children's needs for attention, and if you live far away from your relatives, you may benefit from finding other families with whom you can share parenting responsibilities.

Studies have shown that a harsh, punitive approach to discipline can contribute to sibling rivalry. When parents frequently hit, spank, or yell, children learn that aggressive behavior is the way to solve conflicts. Children who are raised with harsh discipline fight more with each other and also tend to bully other children. A gentle approach to discipline can help prevent both sibling and peer aggression.

Another factor to consider is the lack of private space and toys. Siblings are less likely to fight with each other if each child has some space he can call his own (even if it is only one part of a room) as well as some toys that are exclusively his. If he must constantly share toys and space with his siblings, the number of conflicts will probably increase.

Immaturity can also contribute to sibling rivalry and conflicts over toys. If your child is too young to understand another person's needs and feelings, he will not grasp the concepts of sharing or taking turns. The ability to take another person's perspective gradually increases between the ages of two and eight years, and it is dependent on both brain development and social experiences.

Another reason for fights is frustration caused by inability to accomplish what a sibling can do. Each child has unique gifts and abilities, and siblings tend to compare themselves to each other. Furthermore, children of different ages normally acquire skills at different times, and this discrepancy in abilities can be difficult for a younger sibling to accept. The following example of my own children illustrates this frustration.

> Nicky (age seven) enjoyed playing the piano and learning simple tunes. However, whenever he sat down at the piano and started to play, Sarah (age two) also went to the piano and banged on the keys. I refrained from intervening to see if they could solve this problem by themselves. Nicky tried several approaches, such as giving her turns, playing pieces she could sing along with, or finding something else for her to do, but nothing worked for long. She still bothered him when he played the piano, and he would end up yelling at her. I realized that Sarah felt frustrated because she didn't know how to play the piano, and I decided that they needed my help. The first thing I tried was to help Sarah release her frustration. The next time she bothered her brother at the piano, I held her, lovingly but firmly, to prevent her from doing so. She cried hard in my arms, and after crying, she did not bother him anymore that day. However, the problem would periodically return, so I decided to teach her how to play a simple tune on the piano. She soon enjoyed making up her own little tunes. Once she realized that she, too, could play the piano, she no longer bothered her brother when he played it.

Anything that emphasizes children's different abilities can contribute to sibling rivalry, so try to avoid comparing your children to each other or using praise. A child who does not receive your praise may feel jealous of a sibling who does. It is tempting to compare and praise our children, but it can be harmful to do so. Instead of telling your son that you wish he could get ready for school as quickly as his sister, avoid the comparison, wait until later, and then discuss with him how to speed up the morning routine.

Also try to avoid any behavior that your children could perceive as an unfair privilege for a sibling. This may be difficult if one of your children has special physical or emotional needs. Minimizing competition and contests will also help decrease rivalry (as described in Chapter 4).

Pent-up stress is an important, but often unrecognized, cause of sibling fights. Children often fight with each other so they can have a pretext for releasing pent-up feelings. A boy who has been teased at school may come home and re-enact the teasing with his sister in an effort to heal. His unconscious goal may be to make her so angry that she hits him. He will then have a valid reason to begin crying. So if your children's fights often lead to tears, it's possible that they are provoking each other with the goal of creating an excuse to start crying, although they may not consciously realize what they are doing.

In the following example, a mother described the rivalry between her two children.

> They scream a lot at each other. They get angry about all kinds of things. She gets so frustrated when he teases her. A lot of the rivalry is over toys that they both want to play with at the same time. But when Greg (age five) was away for a week, Julie (age three) still cried a lot. She continued to have temper tantrums even when everything was revolving totally around her and her needs. She would throw herself on the middle of the kitchen floor and scream. It definitely showed me that she just needed to have these tantrums. She had to get her daily quota of crying!

Factors contributing to sibling rivalry

- Lack of attention from parents
- Harsh discipline
- Lack of private space or toys
- Inability to understand others' feelings and needs
- Different abilities among siblings
- One child has special privileges or receives more praise
- Competitive home environment
- Pent-up stress and the need to cry

How can I intervene when my children fight with each other?

You may wonder when and how to intervene during your children's fights. Or perhaps you think it's best to stay out of their fights entirely and let them solve their own problems. There are times when it can be beneficial, or even important, to intervene, and other times when you can wait a little to see if your children can work it out themselves. There is some research evidence that total nonintervention into sibling fights does result in less fighting. However, this outcome occurs at a huge cost, because there is a risk that one child will establish superiority over another, and the chronically defeated child becomes intimidated and stops defending herself (a phenomenon called "learned helplessness"). This situation does not benefit either child.

Try to avoid an authoritarian approach in which you send each child to his or her room, threaten punishment, or promise a reward if they can get along with each other. It is also best to avoid acting as arbiter or judge and imposing your own solution on them in an authoritarian manner. It always takes two people to fight, and the obvious aggressor is not always the one to blame. Her brother or sister may have quietly provoked her by teasing. For this reason, it is rarely helpful to ask who started it.

If your children are playfully wrestling with each other (rough-and-tumble play), there is no need to intervene. However, if they are really hurting each other, I recommend immediate intervention by stepping between them or firmly restraining the one who is about to hit the other. You can then acknowledge their feelings, and one or both may need to cry. The goal is to stop the violence, but not necessarily the noise. Loud, angry crying may be exactly what they need to do.

If your children frequently fight over toys, you may be tempted to establish a rule for these kinds of conflicts. For example, your rule might be the child who has the toy first gets to keep it as long as she wants. This approach can work, but you may be missing an opportunity to help your children think about each other's needs and learn conflict-resolution skills. Children usually don't like a parent's solution anyway and may complain that it's not fair. Furthermore, it's not always clear who had the toy first.

If your children are calm enough to talk and listen, you can help them find a solution through mediation. First give each child a chance to explain what happened, what she needs, and how she feels. After listening to each child, reflect back what you heard, or ask the other child to do so. After you have listened carefully to each child, summarize the conflict, for example, "You two have a problem. John is angry because Karen keeps trying to take the fire engine away. Karen is upset because she was playing with it first and hadn't finished. She left for only a few seconds, and when she came back, John was playing with it. You both want to play with the fire engine at the same time. Can you think of a way to solve your problem?" Be sure to avoid taking sides while describing the conflict in this manner.

With this kind of support, children often find their own creative solutions. When they don't, you can suggest possible solutions (such as taking turns or playing together), and ask if they agree. Mediation with young children requires time and effort, but it helps them learn to identify their own feelings and needs, and think about those of the other person. These are important conflict-resolution skills.

How to do mediation with children

- Allow each child to explain what happened and express emotions.

- Reflect back each child's feelings, or ask the children to do so.

- Describe the conflict without taking sides.

- Invite the children to help think of possible solutions.

If the children are not calm enough for mediation, or if the conflict continues to escalate after mediation, it's possible that one of both of them might need to cry. You can take the toy away and tell them that you cannot let either of them play with it until they work out a solution. This action on your part may trigger some crying and perhaps even anger directed at you. After the children release tensions and frustrations through tears and raging, they may be ready to think of a solution through mediation. If they have agreed to take turns, the child who has to wait for a turn may need to cry while waiting, and you can offer empathy.

If you are feeling energetic, you can try a playful approach. Grab the toy and run away with it, while inviting both children to chase you. This will force them to unite against you in their attempt to retrieve the toy. It may also trigger a healthy release of tensions through laughter, especially if you turn the activity into a power-reversal game and let them catch you. Or you can take the toy and hide it somewhere obvious. Then express mock surprise when they easily retrieve it. Another playful approach is to pretend that you are another child who wants the toy. Complain bitterly that you *never* get a turn and that you haven't played with it for *ages*. Hopefully, all of you will then dissolve into laughter.

Three ways to intervene when two children want the same toy

• Do mediation.

• Remove the toy and encourage crying.

• Use a playful approach and encourage laughter.

Another common problem among siblings is teasing. If your children often tease or criticize each other, they could be imitating adult behavior. The first step would be to make sure that you and other adults in your home do not tease each other or the children. You can also check into other possible causes. Perhaps, without realizing it, you have been favoring one of your children, or maybe one child has excelled at some skill, and her sibling feel less competent. Chronic teasing, criticisms, or interruptions of one sibling by another can also be simply a symptom of jealousy, even when you have not favored one child.

Look for ways to connect with the child who does the teasing, and try to boost her self-esteem and confidence. You can also discuss this issue with your child at a time when she is not teasing her sibling. Another helpful intervention is to encourage the victim to talk directly to his sibling and let her know that he doesn't like what she is doing.

A light, humorous interruption of teasing can help to reduce the habit and promote a release of tensions through laughter, as a mother described in the following example.

Jerry (age five) used to tease Heather (age three) a lot. He would say "doo-doo head" and "diddle dee, diddle dee" just to irritate her. After I discussed this behavior with him, he realized that it was just a bad habit, and I offered to help him stop. We agreed that every time he started to say these obnoxious things to her, I would say, "Cantaloupes, Jerry!" (and Heather has added, "Strawberries!"). It has really worked well, because he would stop teasing her whenever we said these words, and he would actually laugh about it. We didn't have to say "Jerry, don't do that, you shouldn't do that." We didn't have to go through all that put-down of him. He seemed to appreciate that we were reminding him that he just had that habit, and that we were helping him stop it. He didn't feel that we were mad at him or blaming him for it.

How can I remain objective when my children fight?

Most parents find their children's arguments and fights extremely disagreeable. It is painful to see your well-loved children screaming and hurting each other. You may even feel like yelling, hitting, or punishing, even though you know that this response would be counterproductive. You don't want to model the very behavior that you are attempting to stop, but what can you do? You just wish that they could get along with each other. Maybe you feel powerless or incompetent, and wonder if you have failed in some way. You may feel guilty for not loving them enough, not setting proper boundaries, or being a bad role model for them.

To further complicate matters and add to your distress, your children's fights can trigger memories of your own childhood sibling rivalry. Perhaps you have unresolved anger at an older sibling or guilt at having mistreated a younger one. If your parents fought frequently, any fighting in your home can bring up feelings of terror and a compulsive desire to end the argument at any cost. In the following example, a father shared his feelings about his daughter's aggressive behavior toward her younger sister.

When Nancy (age three) hits Sandra (age one) I see red. I get angry, and I feel like hitting. I know it's not good, but that's what I feel like doing. It's my first impulse. Or I shout, and that's not good either. I've been trying to learn to stay calm and listen empathically and all that. I'm a counselor, I ought to be able to do that, but I just get emotional when I see one of my kids hurt by another one of my kids. It's hard for me to control myself. I think it brings back memories of my childhood, of my older sister who used to beat up on me and then get away with it by telling Mom or Dad that I had started it. I still have scars on my arms where my sister scratched and bit me.

If you find yourself becoming frequently angry and overreacting when your children fight, you might benefit from exploring the childhood origins of your anger. Share your memories and feelings with someone who can listen well without judging or giving advice, perhaps your partner, a friend, or a therapist. If you can release these painful emotions by talking, laughing, or crying, you will work through your painful childhood experiences and reduce the likelihood of these emotional triggers. Afterwards, you may find it easier to remain calm and objective when your children fight, and this will allow you to think of more creative and effective solutions.

How can I help my child learn to get along with friends?

Your child's relationship with her friends differs from her relationship with her siblings because she doesn't have to compete with her friends for your attention. Nevertheless, children can have conflicts even with their best friends. Young children do not always act tactfully, and they sometimes talk rudely to their friends. It is not uncommon to hear a child say "I don't want to play with you" or "I'm not your friend anymore." Five minutes later, the two may be playing happily together again! These blunt statements reflect children's momentary, but intense, feelings of anger or irritation with each other. There is no need to intervene or make an issue of such interactions.

When a disagreement arises during play, and if the children do not seem able to solve the problem by themselves, you can do mediation (as described in a previous section). The following example describes how I used mediation to help my daughter and her friend solve a conflict.

> Sarah (age six) and Helen (age five) were playing with dolls one day when I heard them crying and screaming at each other. This behavior was unusual, so I asked them what was going on. They each had a different idea of what a specific doll should wear to a doll party they were planning. This conflict was obviously an important issue for them, and they had not been able to reach a solution. After giving each of them a chance to talk, I reflected back each girl's feelings: "Sarah, you want her to wear the green outfit because it is perfect for a hot day, and Helen, you want the white outfit because the green one is not fancy enough for a party. Can you two think of a solution that works for both of you?" Helen said, "We can't agree because we each want something different," and started to dress the doll in the white dress. Sarah grabbed the doll from her, and there was more screaming and crying. Then I tried suggesting solutions, but they rejected my ideas. Finally, I said, "I'm going to let you two work this out by yourselves. I think you can find a solution that you will both be happy with." I left them alone for a few minutes and heard no more screaming. When I returned, they showed me the doll who was wearing both outfits at once (something I never would have thought of)! They were both happy with this solution and seemed proud at having solved their conflict.

Aggressive behavior is usually an indication of painful feelings. The child who frequently hits or bites other children may be feeling insecure, hurt, angry, or scared. As with sibling fights, these pent-up emotions may be related to the relationship itself (for example, jealousy), or they may have more to do with unrelated stress or unhealed trauma. The aggressive child will probably need help to express her feelings in ways that do not hurt other children. Setting a limit and encouraging the child to cry or rage will help to alleviate the problem. In the following example, a preschool teacher described how he used this approach at the school where he worked.

> At school, very often two children will be fighting over a toy, and if they're both holding onto a toy and struggling with it for a few seconds, the next move on a lot of children's part is to bite or hit to get that toy. If I am close enough, I just reach in between them, put my hand between them, and say "no." Or sometimes, when the child is just ready to strike the blow, or has his mouth open and his teeth poised over the other child's ear lobe or wrist, I just grab him gently and restrain him from going any farther. Then flood gates open, and tears just pour out. All of that intensity and all of that emotion at the moment are released just because of that restraint, that one simple restraint (either saying "no" or just holding him back). And that will often lead into a long crying session. There is usually no trace of aggression after the child has cried.

When your child fights with a friend, the fact that you are not the other child's parent may constrain what you do. If your child has frequent conflicts with a friend at your home, you can discuss intervention strategies with the other child's parents. They may not fully understand or feel comfortable with an approach that encourages crying or raging. To avoid conflicts with the other parents in that case, you will need to use the other two options for dealing with conflicts: either mediation or a playful approach with laughter.

How can I protect my child from sexual abuse?

The sexual abuse of children is a widespread reality and has been happening for hundreds of years. The worldwide prevalence of child sexual abuse is approximately 20% . People who are sexually abused during childhood are more likely to suffer later on from both physical and mental health problems, including obesity, anorexia, depression, anxiety, and substance abuse.

You can help your child resist sexual assault by avoiding the use of authoritarian discipline. Children who have been punished for disobedience may become more easily intimidated and less likely to resist someone who tries to abuse them.

Show respect for your child's body and establish a family rule that nobody touches another person's body without their permission. Obviously, you will need to touch your child for caregiving routines and possible medical reasons, but you can do this respectfully and give your child a chance to indicate when she is ready. Also remember that your child does not owe anybody a hug. Never force her to hug or kiss another person, even grandma, who might expect a thankyou hug after giving your child a present. It's better to respect your child's boundaries and let her decide how she wants to express appreciation.

It's also important to give your child information. Tell her that some adults do hurtful things to children and touch private parts of their body. Let her know that it is okay to say "no," run away, and tell you what happened. You may need to correct your child's mistaken notion that bad people look evil. She needs to know that adults she knows can hurt her, even teachers and family members. There is no need to limit your discussion to sexual abuse. You can also give your child information about kidnapping.

When you discuss these difficult topics with your child, try to be straight-forward without transmitting your own fears, just as you would teach your child how to cross a street safely. You want your child to be well-informed and aware of dangers, but you don't want her to feel too terrified to be away from you. If you yourself have been sexually abused, you could risk transmitting your fear to your child. Any counseling or therapy you can obtain to work through your own trauma will benefit both you and your child.

Any time you and your child see another child being treated hurtfully (for example, being spanked in a supermarket), you can tell your child that you do not agree with what the other adult is doing. If you have the courage actually to intervene lovingly with the other parent, you will become a powerful role model for your own child, who will then be more likely to stand up for herself when an adult tries to abuse her. An effective way to intervene with an angry parent is to say, "It looks like you're having a hard time with your child. Is there something I can do to help?" And then simply listen.

If you feel uncomfortable leaving your child with someone because you have a uneasy feeling about the person, *trust your own feelings*, even if he is a member of your own family. Be particularly wary of men who describe little girls in sexual terms, such as "she's got sexy eyes" or "she would look good in a bikini." These comments may indicate that the man sees the child as a potential sex object. Avoid daycare centers, schools, or after-school programs that do not allow you to drop in and visit your child at any time. If your child is invited to a friend's home, make sure you know and trust the adults who will be responsible for her.

Look for symptoms of sexual abuse. The most obvious clues would be a sudden preoccupation and interest in genitals, excessive masturbation, or drawings of genitals. A sexually abused child may begin talking about sex acts or acting them out with dolls or friends in an attempt to understand what has happened. Signs of being uncomfortable with someone who was formerly trusted can also be an indication of sexual assault.

Be aware that any change in a child's behavior can also be an indication of sexual abuse: regression in toileting habits, bedwetting, withdrawal, clinging behavior, sudden shyness or fearfulness, new behavior problems, loss of appetite, nightmares or sleep disturbances, or resistance to school, being left alone, or playing with friends. The child may simply cry more than usual or resort to repressing mechanisms such as thumb sucking. If any of these symptoms occur without any obvious cause (such as the birth of a sibling, a move, or the parents' divorce), it is wise to check into the possibility of sexual abuse.

If you discover that your child has been sexually abused, realize that it is neither her fault nor yours. Adults who abuse children find devious ways to gain children's confidence and to intimidate them (sometimes with threats), and these abusers can succeed with their plans even with children who are not easily intimidated. It's important to believe your child and let her know that she did the right thing by telling you. Be sure to tell her that it was not her fault. She also needs reassurance that you will protect her and take action so that it will not happen again.

The next step would be to notify the police or a child protection agency. It is important that the child be protected from further abuse and that the offender be confronted. This may be especially difficult for you to do if the offender is a family member, teacher, or friend. You can let your child know that the goal is not to punish the person, but to make sure he gets the help he needs so he will not repeat the hurtful behavior with another child.

Your own feelings may range from shock and disbelief to fear, guilt, or anger. You may need to cry and rage, but it is best to release your emotions away from your child, preferably with a counselor or therapist. You deserve all the support you can get.

Your child will also benefit from therapy. She may need to talk, cry, and rage, and perhaps act out the abuse through play. A competent therapist who has experience working with child sexual assault victims can be helpful. It is not a sign of weakness or failure to seek professional help when needed.

What about children's sex play with each other?

Young children sometimes like to play naked together and inspect each other's genitals. This activity usually takes the form of watching each other urinate or defecate or "playing doctor" together. This kind of play is usually accompanied by much giggling.

Children's sex play serves two major purposes. First of all, it helps children acquire information about human physiology and sex differences. Children are naturally curious about their bodies, and they want to see how their own bodies differ from those of other children.

Secondly, this kind of play can be therapeutic because it allows children to release embarrassment through laughter. Many adults find the topic of sex to be somewhat embarrassing, and parents can unknowingly pass on this feeling to their children. Your child will notice if you seem uncomfortable answering some of his questions or if you avoid the topic altogether. This reaction on your part will probably increase his curiosity about sex and genitals, and it will also transmit your embarrassment to him. Children typically laugh while playing naked together, and this tension-release mechanism helps them overcome their embarrassment.

There is no need to be concerned about this kind of play, provided the children are not hurting or forcing each other in any way. This play is a normal stage that children go through, and it lasts until their curiosity is satisfied and their embarrassment is relieved. If you shame your child or try to ban such play, he will probably find a way to do it secretly.

However, you may need to set some limits for safety and hygiene. Tell your children not to put any objects in their anuses or vaginas, and insist that they wash their hands before and after touching their genitals. If your child's sex play involves children other than his own siblings, you will need to discuss it with the other parents and come to an agreement about how all of you want to handle it.

Even though sex play is normal, it's important to be aware of your child's sex play because it can indicate sexual abuse trauma, as mentioned in the previous section. Children who have been sexually abused may attempt to use sex play to understand what happened and work through the emotions. If your child's sex play seems especially obsessive or secretive, or if it goes beyond "playing doctor" and involves attempts at re-enactment of adult sexual behavior, it would be a good idea to check into the possibility of sexual abuse.

Sex play can be harmful if your child is younger, smaller, or weaker than the other child, or if the other child is suffering from sexual abuse trauma. If another child intimidates your child during sex play and forces him to do uncomfortable things, you will need to intervene in order to stop the play. As a general guideline, it's wise to monitor especially closely any sex play between two children with an age difference of three years or more, or any time you feel uneasy about it.

How can I help my stepchild adjust to me?

It is not within the scope of this book to discuss all the issues involved in divorce, co-parenting after divorce, or step-parenting. Because of the high prevalence of divorces followed by remarriages, however, this section addresses one aspect of this issue. Many parents today face the challenge of step-parenting in a blended family. It is not easy to raise a child who is not your own, especially if you already have children from a previous marriage.

One factor that can prevent a smooth transition to a blended family is that most children are deeply affected by their parents' separation or divorce. The children's feelings can range from mild annoyance to deeper feelings of anger, grief, anxiety, insecurity, confusion, and guilt. The period preceding the separation may have been one of extreme tension in the family and perhaps even violence, with little attention for the children. You and your ex-partner may still feel considerable anger at each other, and perhaps even mistrust. Because of these emotions, your child may experience considerable difficulty adjusting to your divorce. Anything you can do to help your child during and after your divorce will facilitate her later adaptation to a step-parent and to step-siblings. So be sure to allow your child to express emotions and to cry and rage as much as she needs to.

If a stepchild later joins your family, don't expect to have an immediate warm and loving relationship with her. Relationships take time, and your stepchild needs to build up trust. She may still be suffering from the trauma of her parents' divorce, and may feel resentful or angry that you are replacing her real mother or father. So don't be surprised if she expresses anger directly at you, and try not to take it personally. As with your own child after divorce, you can encourage your stepchild to express her feelings.

In the following example, a woman described how she helped a three-year-old boy work through his anger at her.

When I started living with Matthew and his son, Carlos, the new living situation was difficult at first. Carlos resented me being there instead of his mother, and he told me repeatedly to go away in an angry tone of voice. The first few times he said this, I left him alone and went to my room. But after several days of hearing him say "go away" and "I hate you" every time he saw me, I realized that I couldn't disappear from sight every time he was around. So one day I stayed in the living room, and Carlos came over and started pushing and shoving at my legs while saying, "Go away, go away." I said, "No, I'm going to stay here." He pushed me and yelled at me with intense anger while his father sat close by. After a while we all sat on the floor with Carlos between us pushing with all his strength at me with his arms, and at his father with his feet. He seemed to like the resistance and continued to scream and cry. If we moved too far away, he scooted over so he could push at us again. I reassured Matthew that it was good for Carlos to release his anger in this manner. This behavior continued for over an hour, while Carlos cried and yelled, "Go away, I hate you!" to each of us in turn and pushed at us with his hands and feet. Finally I got tired and left. The next day, he started saying again, "I hate you" and began pushing at me, so his father and I spent another hour paying attention to him while he released his anger. It happened again a few times the following week, but after that he never again said that he hated me. We've become good friends. Now Carlos always runs to me and gives me a big hug when he sees me!

Try to avoid the temptation to gain your stepchild's love by giving her presents. Instead, you can establish a loving connection by playing with her. A good activity to begin with is nondirective, child-centered play. Simply sit on the floor with her while she plays, and give her your full attention. Let her direct the play and even tell you what to do. Another helpful form of play might be a pillow fight in which you fake weakness and let her knock you down (power-reversal game). You can also encourage laughter by acting silly together (nonsense play). Separation games (such as hide and seek) can help your stepchild cope with fear of abandonment, which is common in children following divorce. Finally, using a playful approach to discipline will increase your stepchild's willingness to cooperate. These moments of play and laughter will help both of you feel more connected to each other.

Research has shown, not surprisingly, that children after divorce have fewer behavioral and emotional problems when their parents have fewer conflicts. It is therefore important for all the parents involved to resolve their conflicts as amicably as possible and to do their arguing away from the children. Try to avoid involving your stepchild in disputes between you, your new partner, and the child's other parent. Don't ask the child to be an informant about her other parent or an intermediary between you. This guideline also applies to your own children and your relationship with your ex-partner. Children will thrive better after divorce when the adults communicate directly with each other. It is also important to avoid criticizing a child's other parent, no matter how angry you feel or how incompetent you think he or she is. Don't forget that your child probably loves and identifies with that parent, so when you criticize that person, you are indirectly criticizing the child.

There is no need to feel guilty if you do not immediately love your stepchild or if she does not respond at first to your efforts to connect with her. As with any difficult parenting situation, you would probably benefit from finding someone who can listen to you express your feelings.

Exercises

Explore your childhood

1. If you have siblings, describe your relationship with them as a child. Did you fight or argue? If so, how do you feel about the way your parents handled these conflicts?

2. Did you have a best friend as a child (outside of your family)? Describe your friend. What did you enjoy doing together? Did you ever argue or fight?

3. Were you ever sexually abused? If so, have you had a chance to work through the trauma with a competent therapist?

Express your feelings about your child

1. How do you feel about your child's relationship with siblings (if you have more than one child)? Do your children argue or fight with each other? Does their fighting trigger a painful childhood memory? If there are frequent conflicts, what do you feel like doing? (This is not necessarily what you *should* do!)

2. How do you feel about your child's friends? Does your child argue or fight with them? How does it make you feel? Do you feel that your child acts too bossy or too intimidated around other children? If so, how does it make you feel?

3. Are you fearful or mistrustful of other adults who care for your child? Do you suspect that your child is being (or has been) sexually abused? How do you feel about that, and what do you need to do?

Nurture yourself

1. If you have siblings, what is your relationship like now? Do you feel disconnected from them, resentful, or angry? If so, think about what you can do to re-establish a loving connection. Is there something you need to say to improve your relationship?

2. Do you have enough friends? If not, try to make a new friend or renew contact with an old one.

3. Is there tension in your relationship with your partner? If so, think about what you can do to strengthen your connection.

4. If you feel stressed because of co-parenting after divorce or raising stepchildren, find someone to listen to you while you explore your feelings.

Chapter 7

Eating and Ailments

THIS CHAPTER DISCUSSES some typical problems and behaviors that involve children's health and development, including eating habits, hyperactivity, doctor visits, physical pain, and hospital stays. This chapter is not intended as a substitute for medical treatment. If your child shows symptoms of pain, illness, eating disorders, hyperactivity, or any serious emotional or behavior problem, you are strongly advised to consult with a doctor. You can play an important role by supplementing medical treatment with empathy for your child's emotions.

What can I do about eating problems?

Many parents experience conflicts with young children about food. We want our children to eat a balanced diet and be healthy, but their idea of what to eat is often very different from our goals for them. Perhaps you worry because your two-year-old eats practically nothing or your five-year-old continually craves sweets. Maybe you wonder how much to intervene. Should you let your child skip breakfast? Should you restrict sweets? What if she refuses to eat vegetables? An understanding of child development and the psychology of eating can help to answer these questions, alleviate your concerns, and prevent food-related conflicts.

First of all, a rigid schedule of three meals a day may not be the best fit for your child. Young children typically prefer smaller, more frequent meals than older children and adults. They can also meet their nutritional needs with less food than many people realize.

Another important fact is that children will spontaneously select a nutritionally balanced diet when we give them the freedom to choose which foods to eat. Their diet may look very unbalanced for a day or two, but over the period of a week, their food intake will contain all the necessary nutrients. A child may prefer foods high in protein at one meal (or for several days) and foods high in carbohydrates or fats at another time. You can trust your child to select a healthy, balanced diet, and there is no need to worry if it isn't nutritionally balanced at each meal.

One day, my five-year-old daughter wanted nothing but sweet potatoes for dinner, even though I also offered her some meat loaf and broccoli. Another day, she wanted nothing but cheese. I realized that, in any given week, she actually obtained a balanced diet containing adequate amounts of protein, carbohydrates, fats, and vitamins, and she kept herself very healthy with this eating pattern.

Parents can inadvertently cause eating problems in children. Restricting access to certain foods can backfire because restriction increases desire. When parents limit their children's access to specific foods, studies have shown that the children's desire for those foods actually *increases*, and their ability to self-regulate decreases. When children are allowed to eat formerly restricted foods, they will typically eat beyond a feeling of fullness and consume more calories than their bodies need. This unbalanced eating behavior will continue as long as children fear that the foods will again become restricted. When parents continue to avoid all food restrictions, most children eventually become self-regulated and eat less of the formerly restricted foods.

Food should never be used as a reward, and it is especially risky to use sweet foods as a reward for eating other foods, because such a consequence can interfere with children's ability to pay attention to internal feelings of hunger and fullness. Studies have shown that the promise of a reward tends to make children dislike whatever they need to do to earn it. So when you promise your child ice cream if she first eats spinach, you will probably increase her dislike of spinach and increase her craving for ice cream! In the future, she may be even less likely to eat spinach than before.

Another consideration is the use of food to repress emotions. If you repeatedly encourage your child to eat when she is feeling hurt, sad, frightened, or angry (and not really hungry), you will teach her to use food for comfort. This habit could lead to overeating, because she may lose touch with what her body really needs. If your child eats for comfort, she may continue to do so even if you don't interfere with her food choices in any of the other ways described in the chart below.

Parenting practices that can interfere with children's healthy food choices

• Making a hungry child wait for food

• Restricting what or how much a child eats

• Coaxing or forcing a child to eat

• Making a child feel guilty for eating or not eating

• Criticizing or punishing a child for eating or not eating

• Praising or rewarding a child for eating

• Using food as a reward or withholding food as a punishment

• Commenting on the child's weight or body size

• Using food to comfort a child who is hurt, sad, frightened, or angry

---

Increasing numbers of doctors and psychologists recommend that parents use a self-demand approach to feeding, which implies refraining from controlling what their children eat. This self-demand approach allows children to recognize sensations of hunger and fullness, become self-regulated, and make healthy food choices. If your child is seriously overweight or underweight, or suffers from other chronic medical conditions, I recommend that you consult with your child's doctor before implementing the self-demand feeding approach described in the following sections. There are rare medical conditions that can make it difficult for children to regulate their calorie intake appropriately.

How can I implement the self-demand feeding approach?

To implement the self-demand approach, simply let your child decide when, what, and how much he wants to eat. Teach your child to recognize the sensation of hunger by asking him if he is hungry. If he responds "yes," tell him what foods are available (including sweet foods), and ask him what he wants to eat. Younger children may find it easier to determine what their body needs if they can actually see the food choices (rather than simply hear you list them). So I recommend showing a younger child the available food choices when he expresses hunger. After your child has named (or pointed to) the foods he wants, offer him as much as he wants.

The food choices should include at least one food high in protein, one high in carbohydrates, and one high in fat, as well as fruits and vegetables. Don't forget to offer something sweet at the same time that you offer other foods. For example, you might offer your child a slice of cheese, some crackers, peanut butter, ice cream, left-over pasta, a carrot, and a banana. The self-demand approach to feeding requires that you avoid praising or criticizing what your child eats. In fact, there is no need to talk about the food at all, except to ask him if he wants more or if he is full.

This approach does not require you to cook a full meal for your child whenever he declares hunger. You can continue to prepare whatever meals you normally prepare for yourself and other family members. If your child wants to eat before or after these mealtimes, offer him simple snacks or left-overs from a previous meal. If your family is vegetarian, there is no need to buy meat for your child if you offer a variety of other foods rich in protein. Your child's allergies or other medical conditions might also restrict what foods you give him. But it's important to offer your child a variety of foods from the ones that he is allowed to have and give him control over what and when he eats.

Many young children prefer a limited diet of a few favorite foods, and they resist anything new. Children are more willing to try new foods if they have participated in shopping for ingredients and cooking. If you have a garden, your child may enjoy eating vegetables that he has helped grow. You can also use a playful approach to encourage your child to taste novel foods, but don't force the issue. Studies have shown that any kind of parental coercion is associated with more food refusals by children. Your child will try new foods when he feels ready to do so.

Some children refuse foods combined with others (such as in a casserole), even though they might eat each ingredient separately. Others develop an aversion to certain foods because of appearance or texture. Pepper on food "looks dirty," parsley "tickles," and bread crusts are "too hard." Your child may prefer specific foods because of their play or symbolic value. He may request a slice of cheese rather than a chunk of the same cheese, so he can create animal shapes by taking bites out of the slice (as my daughter enjoyed doing). A child who has a baby sibling may want to eat foods similar in texture to those that the baby eats. There is no harm in catering to these whims, aversions, and preferences.

Food binges are also normal during early childhood. One hot summer, my six-year-old son wanted to eat granola and yoghourt several times a day, and not much else. He enjoyed serving himself these two foods whenever he wanted, and he maintained excellent health and normal weight gain on that unusual diet. I recommend keeping a list of your child's current favorite foods and making sure that you always have those on hand.

You may find it difficult to implement this self-demand approach to feeding, especially if you were not raised this way. If your parents controlled what you ate as a child, you may feel that you need to control your child in the same way. Keep in mind that your parents' approach to feeding, although well-intentioned, may have led you to ignore your own body's signals of hunger or fullness. This could make it difficult for you to trust your child's food choices. When you begin to implement this approach with your child, you might benefit from giving *yourself* more freedom to pay attention to your body's hunger signals.

In the following example, a mother reported how difficult it was for her to maintain a relaxed attitude about her daughter's eating habits.

> My self-esteem is directly linked to what Angie (age four) puts into her mouth. The other day she was looking for popsicles in the freezer, and she discovered some frozen vegetables in a bag, and said, "Let's have some of these." It was three o'clock in the afternoon, and I almost fell over from surprise. Of course I cooked them up and served them to her, and she actually ate them! I felt that I had finally succeeded as a mother because my child actually ate something I prepared that was good for her. At other times, when she doesn't eat what I think is good for her, or doesn't finish what's on her plate, I try very hard not to say anything, or to let on that it's important to me. But secretly, I'm a wreck inside because she doesn't eat what I wish she would eat.

What about candy?

Many parents find themselves in a dilemma about candy. Even though you want your child to become self-regulated, you may wonder if the self-demand approach applies to candy. Perhaps you fear that your child would eat nothing but candy and would become ill, gain weight, or ruin her teeth. To complicate matters, our culture practically worships sweets. We give candy as gifts, save it for special treats, and even use it as a reward. Many holiday traditions include traditional sweets. Colorful and attractive candy is always placed within children's reach in supermarkets. With this degree of exposure and cultural conditioning, it would be surprising if children did *not* crave candy.

Some parents try to solve the candy dilemma by banning it completely, while others limit their children's candy consumption to special occasions (such as birthdays or Halloween). Another approach is to allow one piece of candy per day. Because of the craving that can result from any kind of food restriction, I recommend the self-demand approach, which implies maintaining a supply of candy in your home and letting your child eat as much as she wants. When candy has the same status as carrots or bananas, it eventually loses its appeal.

In the following example, a mother described the negative effects of her own mother's restriction of sweet foods.

> Candy and cookies were very strictly regulated in our home. I used to get in trouble for eating them. My mother never said, "Who ate the cookies?" but rather "Who *stole* the cookies?" It was that wonderful thing I could do to be naughty. To this day, if I see a cookie, I *have* to eat it. It's the criminal in me coming out. I have to see if I can get away with it. After church, when they have a pile of cookies out there, I can feel my adrenaline going all out, and I have to eat as many as I can get my hands on! I'm overweight now because I just gained 30 pounds over the Christmas season from all the sweets I ate.

If you have been restricting candy, your child will probably binge on it for several weeks when you first implement this approach. But after she trusts that she will always have an unlimited supply, she will eventually stop eating candy and begin paying attention to her body's real food needs. Here is my experience with the self-demand approach.

> With both of my children, I used the self-demand approach to feeding from birth on, *except for candy*. I felt uncomfortable letting them eat as much candy as they seemed to want, so I restricted their consumption to one piece per day. But I eventually grew tired of monitoring them, so I told

them one day (with some trepidation) that there would be no more limits and they could eat as much candy as they wanted. I found the courage to let them select candy at the store, and I bought whatever they pointed to. Sarah (age six) binged on candy for about two months. After that, to my amazement, her candy consumption gradually decreased, even though she still had an unlimited supply. Interestingly, she became increasingly selective about the kind of candy she liked. She started telling me that certain kinds were too sweet or smelled bad. Nicky (age eleven) never binged on candy, but regulated himself quite reasonably from the start. As adults, neither of my children eats much candy, and neither has ever been overweight.

When you first start to allow unlimited candy in your home, it's important to make other foods readily available. If your child can easily find the candy but must make more of an effort to eat cheese or an apple, she will probably eat candy when her body needs calories. I recommend having plates of ready-to-eat, bite-sized foods in plain sight at all times, such as crackers, slices of fruits or vegetables, and slices of cheese. An especially important time to make these wholesome foods visible and available is when your child arrives home from school or daycare. If she doesn't immediately see these food options, she will probably reach for the candy.

You will need to decide how far you want to go with the self-demand approach. I allowed candy, as described above, but I decided to keep foods high in unhealthy fats out of our home (such as potato chips and commercial pastries). Instead, I bought or made healthy alternatives for my children. The important thing is to let your child have free choice among the foods that you have decided to allow in your home.

What if my child uses food to suppress emotions?

The self-demand approach to feeding will only work well if you combine it with the other suggestions in this book, especially those about allowing your child to cry. As I mentioned earlier in this chapter, when we use food to comfort a child who is hurt, sad, frightened, or angry, we can cause him to lose touch with what he really needs. This problem can begin during infancy, especially when parents don't know about the importance of stress-release crying and misread their baby's cues. If you interpreted every cry as a hunger signal, you probably offered your breast or a bottle to soothe your baby even when you had recently fed him. He may have acquired a habit of eating to repress painful emotions (a control pattern), and he may think he is hungry whenever he needs to cry. His body will remember that breast milk (or formula) was very sweet, so he may be especially attracted to sweet foods whenever he feels upset and needs to cry.

If your child overeats to numb painful emotions, the most effective approach, in the long run, is to address his underlying feelings instead of trying to control what he eats. Just like a thumb sucking habit, overeating is a control pattern that he does to his own body to repress emotions. If your child eats for comfort and is overweight, you can implement the self-demand approach described in this chapter. But I recommend that you also look for ways to help him regain the ability to cry. Do you try too hard to keep him happy at all times? Do you distract him from crying? Are you talking too much instead of listening? Are you missing "broken-cookie" moments (small pretexts that trigger a tantrum)? Does your fear of a meltdown make you hesitant to set limits?

If you restrict what your overweight child eats, he may develop even more of a craving for comfort foods. Instead, try to help him pay attention to his body and emotions. If he compulsively eats one cookie after another, you can ask him the following questions: "Are you really hungry? Are you sure you want another cookie? Shall we cuddle and talk? Are you upset about something?" You could also suggest the following: "Would you like to hold a cookie while we talk and cuddle for a while? Then you can decide if you still want to eat it." Letting him hold a cookie will reassure him that you are not trying to restrict how many he eats. Make sure that other foods are as easily accessible as the cookies at all times, as described in the previous section.

You can also use humor and laughter to help your child overcome compulsive eating. Grab the cookies and run away with them, but let your child chase and catch you, and then surrender them with exaggerated reluctance. Pretend that *you* are starved for cookies, and ask your child to hide them so you won't eat too many. Then act frantic as you desperately search for them and fail to find them. Get down on your knees and beg your child to give you one. Or pretend to be a cookie and make it say, "Ouch, you bit me!" whenever your child takes a bite of it. Anything to get your child to laugh will help him release the anxiety or other painful emotions that lie at the root of his compulsive eating habit. He may actually surprise you by forgetting to eat cookies while doing these playful activities with you.

Children can also use food as a way to gain your attention when they feel disconnected. A child who overeats may simply need more attention. If you often comment on what he eats and try to restrict him, he may overeat to force you to pay attention to him. On the other hand, a child could refuse to eat in order to attract your attention and keep you involved with him. These behaviors are more likely to occur if your child has one or more younger siblings who require much of your attention. If your child eats too much or too little as a way of attracting your attention, stop commenting on what he eats. Offer him food, then let him decide what and how much to eat. Give him more attention at other times so he won't need to use inappropriate eating behavior to make you notice him. Schedule child-centered play sessions with him a few times a week.

Try to become aware of your *own* eating habits. Are you a good role model? Do you overeat? Do you reach for your favorite comfort foods when you are stressed, depressed, lonely, or frustrated? Do you go on diets only to regain the weight back later on? If you suffer from eating or weight problems, your child may imitate your behavior. You will benefit from exploring your childhood eating experiences and becoming aware of the emotions that you are trying to numb by eating. Find someone who can listen to you express your emotions.

How can I deal with behavior problems during mealtimes?

Mealtime behavior problems have several possible causes. Children are especially resistant to being told to finish everything on their plate, and their behavior may reflect this resentment. They might yell, throw food on the floor, leave the table, or pick a fight with a sibling. If you let your child eat what she wants, her behavior will probably improve, and mealtimes will become calmer.

If you force your child to sit at the table after she has finished eating and wants to go play, she may act inappropriately. Teach her to excuse herself politely, and let her go play. Also try to make family mealtimes enjoyable for everybody so she will *want* to sit at the table. Some families have a ritual for sharing feelings about the day during the evening meal. For example, each person takes a turn to talk about the best thing and the worst thing that happened that day. So even if your child isn't hungry, she will probably still want to join the family to participate in the ritual.

Some parents think that children should not play with their food. However, young children have a natural desire to touch their food and play with it. There is nothing inherently wrong with this (assuming their hands are clean!). For some children, the texture of food is just as important as the taste, smell, or visual appearance of it. Others may use food as a creative medium. Your child may enjoy creating a face by placing raisins or other small foods on a round cracker. Consider letting your child finger paint with mashed potatoes or instant pudding. However, you may want to set limits on your child's food play, especially if much of the food ends up on the floor. You may also want to restrict food play in restaurants or at other people's homes.

Mealtime behavior problems sometimes have no relationship to food. Table manners can be a source of conflict between parents and children. You will naturally want to have some rules and expectations for appropriate table manners, but be sure that your rules are realistic and age appropriate. A three-year-old will probably have difficulty using a knife and fork or sitting still for an hour-long dinner party. However, she is probably old enough to learn to keep her feet off the table. Use gentle reminders instead of punishments or rewards, and don't forget to be a good role model.

If your child has pent-up feelings for any reason, she may act inappropriately at mealtimes, simply because it's a moment when she has your attention. If she needs to cry, she will look for a pretext to do so. She may become overly demanding and repeatedly ask for a specific cup, only to reject it and ask for something else. Or she may ask you to do things for her (such as cut up her food) but then criticize the way you do them.

If you feel that your child's demands are becoming unreasonable, it's appropriate to set a limit on what you are willing to do and to say "no" to whatever your child is demanding. ("I'm not going to wash the red cup for you, but here's a clean blue one.") These kinds of limits will probably provide your child with the pretext she needs to burst into tears and release her pent-up feelings.

If you continue to cater to every unreasonable demand when your child needs to cry, you may become exhausted and resentful, and your child will not have an opportunity to release her pent-up stress. She will probably continue her demanding behavior until she has a pretext to start crying. She may even *create* a pretext, as the following example illustrates.

> Two-year-old Willie woke up whiny and fussy. At breakfast he wanted milk on his cereal, so his mother poured some milk on it. Then he complained because he wanted milk to drink in a glass. As there was no milk left, his mother poured some of the milk from the cereal into a glass for him. He immediately poured it back into his cereal dish, but then complained again that he wanted milk to drink. His mother patiently poured some milk back into his glass. He then picked up the glass, looked at his mother, and calmly and deliberately poured the milk onto the floor. Then he began to cry because he didn't have any milk to drink!

In this example, the child was whiny to begin with and obviously needed to cry, but he required a reason to do so. His mother unintentionally prevented him from having a pretext to cry, because she kept giving into his whims. So he deliberately set up a situation that was impossible for his mother to fix. She could have prevented the spilled milk if she had said earlier that there was no milk for him to drink. At that point, he probably would have begun crying, which is what he needed to do.

I have been told that my child has ADHD. What can I do to help him?

If your child is hyperactive, impulsive, or inattentive, he may receive a diagnosis of Attention Deficit Hyperactivity Disorder (ADHD). Most doctors and psychologists consider this to be a medical condition with a biological origin, and the treatment of choice is psychiatric medication. In the U.S., physicians are allowed to prescribe these drugs for children as young as four who meet the diagnostic criteria.

In spite of decades of research, however, the status of ADHD as a medical disorder has not been established. The diagnosis is based exclusively on teachers' and parents' subjective observations. The checklist for diagnosis includes such behaviors as "often does not seem to listen when spoken to directly" and "often avoids, dislikes, or is reluctant to engage in tasks that require sustained mental effort (such as schoolwork or homework)."

A growing number of professionals (including myself) have questioned whether ADHD is a real medical condition with a biological cause, and they disapprove of giving potentially dangerous psychiatric drugs to children. To clarify, nobody doubts that some children act impulsively, have trouble sitting still, or can't seem to pay attention in school. These behaviors are real, and parents and teachers understandably find these children difficult to manage. But there is considerable evidence that environmental, social, educational, developmental, or emotional factors can cause the symptoms that so often result in a diagnosis of ADHD.

Environmental toxins (such as lead exposure) can lead to these symptoms, as can some medical conditions (such as hyperthyroidism). Be sure to obtain a thorough medical exam for your child to rule out these possibilities. There is no evidence that sugar consumption causes the behaviors that lead to a diagnosis of ADHD, but other dietary factors could contribute to your child's symptoms. For example, caffeine is a stimulant that acts directly on the nervous system and can cause agitation, hyperactivity, and insomnia.

Another consideration is your child's educational environment. Would his behavior improve in a school that provides more freedom and allows him to learn through hand-on activities, creativity, movement, and games? Many hyperactive and inattentive children show a surprisingly long attention span during activities that they have freely chosen to do. Also consider the possibility that your child may simply be developing more slowly than other children. Studies have shown that impulse control develops slightly later in boys than in girls. Interestingly, boys are more likely to receive a diagnosis of ADHD than are girls.

Don't overlook the possible impact of stress or trauma. There is strong evidence that children are more likely to receive a diagnosis of ADHD if they have been exposed to poverty, parental divorce, physical or sexual abuse, domestic or neighborhood violence, parental substance abuse or mental illness, or a history of foster care. The neurobiology of trauma can account for all the symptoms of ADHD (including impulsivity, hyperactivity, and inattentive behavior). Children who have distressing experiences, such as those mentioned above, will develop a nervous system that prepares them for danger, and their brain will function differently than the brains of children who have not been exposed to trauma. Traumatized children typically become hypervigilant and quick to respond (impulsive). Hyperactivity can be caused by high levels of stress hormones (such as adrenaline and cortisol), which are chronically elevated in traumatized children. Finally, a tendency to daydream in school (inattentive behavior) could be a symptom of mild dissociation, which is one way that a child's nervous system copes with trauma.

Some studies have found differences in the brains of children diagnosed with ADHD, and these findings have led many people to think that the cause must be biological. But the data doesn't prove that conclusion, because brain structure and function simply reflect how a child uses his brain, which in turn results from past experiences. The underlying cause for the observed neurological differences could be emotional stress or trauma.

Even if your child didn't experience any of the major traumas mentioned above, perhaps he had a difficult birth, early medical interventions, or a traumatic separation from you. If you suspect that stress or unhealed trauma might lie at the root of your child's behavior, begin by looking for sources of stress in his life and ways to reduce these. I also recommend the suggestions in this book for helping him heal from stress and trauma through tears and tantrums as well as play and laughter. In my consulting experience, many parents have reported to me that their children become much calmer and more attentive after a good cry.

A final consideration is that your child's behavior may simply lie within the normal range of human behaviors. Our species has survived and thrived partly because of our neurodiversity. Prehistoric groups needed all kinds of people with different skills, and natural selection would have favored a wide variety of genetic traits. Some people were probably especially skilled at continually monitoring all environmental stimuli and responding quickly to danger. Children with those traits today might receive a diagnosis of ADHD. Other people were probably better at calmly focusing on a single task and reflecting more deeply about long-term survival strategies. Today, children with those traits are especially good at sitting still and paying attention in school.

In conclusion, the behaviors that lead to a diagnosis of ADHD have many possible causes. Even if your child is being treated with psychiatric medication, I urge you to consider these possibilities, especially his school environment and trauma history. You may be able to address these issues in a way that will allow you to reduce his medication or even eliminate it entirely. Also look for your child's strengths. Perhaps he is (or will be) especially good at sports, dance, creative thinking, or quick decision-making during emergencies.

Maybe he has leadership qualities or a unique sense of humor. Because of his ability to notice a variety of stimuli simultaneously, he may be especially skilled at picking up information in his environment without much effort (incidental learning).

How can I help my child cope with dental and medical procedures?

Dental and medical procedures can be stressful, painful, and frightening for children. If possible, find a practitioner who will allow you to be present with your child at all times. You may need to reassure the practitioner that you will not interfere with the procedures and that your child will be cooperative. You are not being overprotective by wanting to stay with your child.

You may wonder how far in advance to let your child know about the appointment. If you tell him too far in advance, he may become increasingly anxious as the day approaches. On the other hand, if you wait until the last minute, or don't warn him at all, he may feel betrayed and angry. One or two days before the appointment is probably sufficient advance notice for young children. This allows time for your child to ask questions, express his feelings, and rehearse the visit through play with you, but it does not give him enough time to dwell on it or to build up a huge amount of apprehension.

It's important to explain clearly to your child the reasons for the procedure. Even young children can understand the need for dental fillings, blood tests, or vaccinations if you base your explanations on concepts that are familiar to them. Although your child has no choice about the procedure itself, try to give him as many other choices as possible. Maybe you can let him decide which parent will take him or which arm to have an injection in.

At home, you can use a playful approach to let your child know what to expect and also help him release anxiety through laughter. Role-playing can be an effective way to accomplish these goals. Use props and take turns playing the roles of the doctor and patient. To elicit laughter, pretend to be terrified when you play the role of the patient. While playing the role of the doctor, pretend to be stupid and incompetent. The following example describes how I used nonsense play to prepare my daughter for a dental appointment.

> At five years of age, Sarah had to go to the dentist for a checkup and teeth cleaning. I had taken her to the dentist the previous year, but she had refused to open her mouth to let the dentist clean her teeth! I assumed that I had not adequately prepared her. This time, I decided that she would arrive fully prepared and knowing exactly what to expect. I told her about the appointment one day ahead of time, and I invited her to do some role-playing about it. She eagerly joined me in a game in which we took turns being the dentist. When I was the dentist, I emphasized the importance of keeping her mouth open and of holding very still. Then I pretended to polish her teeth with an electric polisher, and I made a funny noise. This caused her to laugh, so I made another noise, claiming that I couldn't remember what noise the machine actually made. Together we experimented with a number of different noises. This activity kept her laughing for 15 minutes! The next day at her appointment, she was extremely cooperative, and the dentist had no trouble cleaning her teeth.

Your child may need to cry before, during, or after the procedure. Try to accept his emotions rather than encourage him to be brave. If medical practitioners try to distract your child from crying, you may need to intervene gently by saying, "He needs to know that it's okay to cry here, and it's certainly okay with me if he cries." The practitioners may feel relieved when they understand that you are not expecting them to keep your child happy.

The following example describes a mother's successful preparation of her three-year-old son's vaccination.

> I decided that I would tell him about the injection the day before, so that he would have time to cry about it

if he wanted to. So I told him, and I made it clear that he had no choice. I explained about the bad disease he could get, and I told him that some scientists had found this new vaccine that would help protect him. Well, he immediately said, "No, I'm not going to have it," and he cried for half an hour or so. We got out the doctor kit and one of his favorite stuffed animals, and we pretended that the animal needed the shot, and we let the animal be upset and scared. I told him, "It's alright if you're scared. All you have to do is hold still so it can be over as fast as possible." He still kept saying, "I'm not going to have that injection." Well, the next morning, it was the first thing he mentioned when he woke up. He no longer said he would not have the injection, but rather, "I don't want to have the injection." I said again that it was really important and that he had to have it, and we talked about how long it would hurt. When the time came, I gave him a choice of whether he wanted papa or me (or both of us) to take him, and he chose me. In the car, he was very quiet at first, then he said, "I'm really scared." I said, "It's all right to be scared. But I'm going to be with you, and it's going to be over fast." I really feared that he would refuse to get out of the car. But he didn't! He got out willingly and went into the building. Fortunately, we didn't have to wait very long. The nurse had the syringe in her pocket, so he never really saw it. I was holding him, and he had the injection, and it was over. He didn't cry until after the nurse had left, and then cried some.

Some children develop an intense needle or dentist phobia, even when they have been well prepared ahead of time. A phobia can occur after a traumatic experience that made them feel powerless, such as a painful procedure or a trip to the emergency room. If your child has such a phobia, you could try implementing the suggestions in Chapter 2 to help him overcome it.

How can I help my child deal with physical pain?

Most people find it distressing to see a child in pain, and it's only natural to want to make the pain go away. For intense pain from medical conditions such as an ear infection, a fever headache, or a broken bone, it certainly makes sense to offer your child pain medication if she needs it. You will probably be able to determine your child's pain level by observing her behavior. When your child is old enough, you can let her decide if she wants pain medication.

For minor injuries, however, it is not usually necessary to numb the injured area or use pain medication, even if the child is crying. (An exception would be if ice is needed to prevent inflammation.) An injured child will typically seek the attention of an adult, get physically close, and cry. Your job is to accept the crying. Pain from a small injury can be an important part of your child's learning experience. When you allow your child to feel the pain and to cry, she will be more likely to take necessary precautions in the future so that such an injury won't happen again. When you numb the pain or distract your child's attention from it, this learning may not take place as effectively.

Many parents have reported to me that their children tend to cry harder and longer when the parents give them attention and sympathy after an injury. These parents wonder if they are somehow causing their child to cry more than necessary. I reassure the parents that children never cry more than necessary. Be sure not to overreact, however. If you are panicking, your child will sense your fear and have more to cry about. But if you remain fairly calm, and your child cries more than expected after a minor injury, she may be releasing emotional pain in addition to the physical pain. After a bruised knee from a tricycle accident, your child may feel angry at another child for bumping into her. She may even be angry at the tricycle for tipping over! Or perhaps the accident frightened her. If you allow your child to cry as much as needed, her physical and emotional pain will eventually disappear.

Another reason why crying sometimes seems out of proportion to the amount of physical pain is that children make use of injuries to cry about other things (the "broken-cookie phenomenon," as described in Chapter 1). The scraped knee or cut finger can provide a pretext to release accumulated, pent-up tensions resulting from past distressing experiences. The use of a minor injury as a pretext for a major meltdown is more likely to occur if your child has not cried enough in the past. She will make use of your loving concern to catch up on the crying she needs to do.

Some parents fear that they will teach their child to be a crybaby by encouraging crying after minor injuries. This attitude is more likely to occur with sons than with daughters. The cultural expectation is for boys to be strong, tough, and brave. Try to remember that crying is not an indication of weakness, but a healing mechanism that will benefit boys as much as girls.

Administering first aid remedies for minor injuries can be challenging with young children, especially when they refuse to let anybody touch their injuries. Try to relax and remember that a few minutes delay probably won't make much difference from a medical point of view. When you need to treat an injury (remove a splinter, clean a scraped knee, or apply a bandage), explain what you need to do and then wait until your child is ready. Allow her to cry, and keep reminding her of what you must do. If your child continues to refuse your treatment, give her as many choices as possible. You can also tell her that you will stop immediately when she asks you to. You can even let her run out of the bathroom and come back when she is ready to continue. Depending on her age, she may be able to do some of the wound care herself, such as cleaning a scraped knee.

You can also try a playful approach to help your child release anxiety through laughter. If she continues to refuse all treatment, you will have to administer first aid anyway, calmly but firmly, while allowing her to scream. The younger your child, the more difficult it will be to gain her cooperation. But even two-year-olds can become surprisingly cooperative when we take the time to explain the reasons for treatment, give them some choices, and allow them to cry.

How can I help my child during a trip to the emergency room?

During a medical emergency, your child may be frightened and in pain, and may not cooperate willingly with the doctors and nurses. You yourself may be highly anxious and concerned about your child's well-being. Furthermore, you may not have time to prepare your child, which can add to everybody's stress.

My guidelines are to stay with your child, if possible, and allow him to cry as much as needed. Try to remain calm while explaining everything to him. Give him some choices. If you need to restrain him physically, do so lovingly and explain why this is necessary.

One of the most distressing experiences for a young child is to be left with strangers at a time when the child is frightened and in pain. The following example from a mother I interviewed illustrates the negative consequences of leaving a child alone with doctors and nurses during a medical emergency.

One evening Richard (age four) was running, and he fell and hit his head on concrete. Later on, he said that he couldn't see well, and I got very concerned. I thought he might have a hematoma or something. So I decided to take him to the emergency room. At the last minute, he didn't want to go. He was crying, saying he wasn't going. Well, I told him we had to go. I said it may be nothing, but it might be serious. A young physician was on duty when we got there. Richard started crying and wouldn't let the doctor touch him. The doctor said to me, "We often get more cooperation when parents aren't in the room." Now everything in me said, "No, that's wrong. I can't leave." But I was also scared to death that something was seriously wrong with my child, and I was really at the point of being willing to do anything to make sure that he was okay. So I left the room. Of course he continued to scream, and they had to call in an orderly to help hold him down. Finally, I opened the door and went back in. They had been able to see that he was okay. Well, he was angry at them and angry at me.

I had deserted him. He didn't want me to hold him, and he hit me. He was just so angry that I had left him. They said he seemed to be okay and that we could go home, but he had such a need to regain some control that he refused to leave and began crying because we were leaving. He didn't want to get in the car, and said, "I don't want to go home. I want to live here." So I just waited while he cried some more. Finally he got in the car. But when we got home, he didn't want to get out of the car. He stayed there crying for about ten minutes before he came into the house.

This mother accepted her son's crying and raging, but she realized later that he would have had less to cry about if she had insisted on staying with him in the emergency room. It is understandably difficult to stand up for our children's need for connection in situations such as these, when we ourselves are terrified.

How can I help my child through a stay in the hospital?

Even if you are allowed to stay with your child, a hospital stay can still be traumatic for her. There are several steps you can take to help your child through the experience and minimize the trauma. As with doctor and dentist visits, preparation can reduce your child's anxiety. If it's not an emergency, you will have time to give your child explanations in advance and answer her questions. Be sure to check for possible misconceptions. Your child may have a notion that people go to hospitals only to die. Be honest about the possibility of physical pain. See if you can visit the hospital ahead of time with your child. At home, you can use role-play to give information, and laughter play to help your child release anxiety. Books about children in hospitals can also help.

Your child will be less traumatized if you stay with her in the hospital as much as possible. If you cannot be present the entire time, try to arrange for another trusted adult to be with your child. Important times to be present are during the first night, immediately before and after surgery, during tests or procedures, and at bedtime. Let your child bring a special toy or stuffed animal from home, especially if you can't be with her all the time. Physical contact is especially important during illness and pain, so be sure to touch and hold your child as much as possible. Hold her hand during difficult procedures. Give her massages. Even a foot massage can help a child relax.

Inform yourself about the procedures and treatments, and explain them to your child. Information can help your child feel less anxious, and it may also make her more cooperative. The younger your child, the less likely she will be to understand explanations and to cooperate with the doctors and nurses.

Be vigilant and know your rights. You have the right to see your child's medical records and to know who is examining her and why. You can question the need for procedures or medication. Check any medication that your child receives, and keep an eye on any apparatus hooked up to your child to be sure it is working properly.

Another suggestion is to let your child have as many choices as possible so she can feel less powerless. Perhaps you can ask the nurse to let your child choose which arm to put intravenous fluid in, or maybe she can have a choice of foods. Children past infancy can certainly decide for themselves whether they need pain medication.

Laughter is an important stress-release mechanism and antidote to anxiety. It can also boost the immune system and speed recovery, so anything that makes your child laugh will be beneficial. Studies have found that clown interventions in pediatric hospitals can reduce children's anxiety before surgery.

Be sure to let your child cry as much as needed, but be aware that a very sick child may not have the energy to cry. She can always catch up later, after her energy returns. In the 1960's, researchers made some interesting observations of children in a long-stay orthopedic hospital. The researchers noticed that the children who openly cried and screamed at the beginning of their hospital stay eventually adjusted very well and accepted the medical care and the limitations placed on them. This behavior was strikingly different from that of the children who were so-called "perfect" patients right from the start. Although these children appeared to be calm, cheerful, and cooperative, they were the ones most likely to show signs of stress later on, such as regression to infantile modes of behavior, wetting and soiling, eating or sleeping difficulties, and learning problems. A possible interpretation of these observations is that crying and raging can actually help children adjust to a stressful situation such as a hospital stay. At the very least, this emotional release didn't hurt them or make things worse.

If your child is too sick to laugh or cry, or if she finds it too painful to do so (for example, after abdominal surgery), you can make up stories to lift her mood and distract her from her discomfort. Therapists have found that helpful stories for ill children are ones that feature the child herself as a strong and brave protagonist, and which include humor, adventures, surprises, and magic.

Don't forget to take care of yourself. Try to find someone who can listen when you need to talk or cry. Many hospitals have chaplains on hand who are trained to listen. Researchers have found that when parents have an opportunity to express their feelings about their children's hospitalization, this has a positive influence on their children's emotional state as well as their own. A mother I interviewed told me how she took care of her own need to cry in a hospital.

> Maria was only two-and-a-half years old when she had to have eye surgery. I was very upset when the nurse took her from me and wheeled her into the operating room, and I couldn't help sobbing. I felt the need for someone to be with me, to give me some caring attention while I cried. It was a Catholic hospital, so I asked for a nun. When she came, I asked her to be with me and pray with me while I cried. We went to the chapel, and I cried for at least half an hour while she just held my hand. She said her prayer, and I said my prayer, each in our own way. After that, I felt much better and went back to wait outside the operating room.

After your child returns home, she will benefit from symbolic play with you, which involves the theme of doctors, hospitals, and illness. Give her a toy doctor kit, and let her play the doctor's role while you take the role of a frightened patient. If you can get your child to laugh, the play will be even more therapeutic.

Don't be surprised if your child cries easily after returning home, or if she appears to overreact after minor injuries. This is a common reaction. Your child is using the pretext of the minor injury to release the distress associated with her hospitalization.

How to help a child through a stay in the hospital

- Prepare your child ahead of time, if possible.

- Let your child bring a special toy from home.

- Stay with your child as much as possible.

- Provide physical contact.

- Inform yourself and give your child explanations.

- Be vigilant and know your rights.

- Give your child choices.

- Encourage laughter.

- Allow your child to cry.

- Take care of your own needs.

- Encourage play, laughter, and tears after your child returns home.

Exercises

Explore your childhood

1. How did you feel during mealtimes as a child? Were you ever forced to eat a food that you didn't want, or denied a food that you wanted? How did you feel about that?

2. Were you overweight or underweight as a child? How did you feel about your weight?

3. How did you feel about going to the doctor or dentist as a child? What memories do you have associated with illness, accidents, doctors, dentists, and hospitals?

Express your feelings about your child

1. How do you feel about your child's food preferences? Do you have concerns about using the self-demand approach to feeding your child? What are they?

2. How do you feel when you take your child to a doctor or dentist? Is there anything that makes this difficult for you?

3. Is your child hyperactive, impulsive, or inattentive? Has he been diagnosed with ADHD? How do you feel about this? Could stress or unhealed trauma lie at the root of your child's symptoms? What are your child's strengths?

Nurture yourself

1. Do you eat for comfort when you are depressed, anxious, lonely, or stressed? If so, join a support group that addresses the emotional origins of eating problems.

2. Treat yourself to a food that was forbidden or restricted during your childhood. Enjoy it!

3. Try the self-demand eating approach on yourself for one week, while paying close attention to your body's signals of hunger, food preference, and fullness.

Conclusion

Major themes in this book

There are several important themes running throughout this book, which are relevant to every topic. I have summarized them here.

Children have many legitimate needs

All children require a great deal of individual attention, time and space to play, and a stimulating environment. They need to be listened to, read to, and played with. Other key needs include physical and emotional safety, and exposure to the adult world in doses they can assimilate. Their education should build on their interests and individual learning styles while meeting their needs for choice, discovery, and movement.

Children have intense feelings

They experience the entire range of human emotions, from minor irritations to intense anger, fear, grief, and confusion. Some children are more highly sensitive than others, but all children are vulnerable, easily overwhelmed, and frequently frustrated. Fears are common because of lack of information, their growing imagination, and a new awareness of death. Jealousy between siblings can occur even in the most loving of families.

Children can heal from distressing experiences

Human beings are born with the ability to recover from daily stresses as well as from traumatic experiences that cause pain, terror, sadness, powerlessness, or frustration. The recovery process occurs naturally when children feel safe and connected to a loving adult. They heal from stress and trauma by crying, raging, trembling, talking, playing, and laughing. Children would not flourish if we accepted only their positive feelings and ignored or punished them for expressing sadness, anger, or fear.

Behavior problems always have a valid cause
Children can be disruptive, obnoxious, impatient, demanding, uncooperative, stubborn, rude, destructive, and violent. Three possible reasons account for these behavior problems: the child has an unmet need, lacks information, or is suffering from stress or unhealed trauma. To change these behaviors, we need to look beneath the surface and address the underlying cause.

Children don't need punishments or rewards
Traditional behavioral approaches (with punishments or rewards) can damage the parent/child relationship, make children feel resentful and powerless, and lower their self-esteem. Children do sometimes need loving limits (without punishment), but the goal of discipline is to teach children to think about the long-range consequences of their actions rather than the immediate personal ones. Children benefit when we work *with them* to solve conflicts instead of doing things *to them* in order to change their behavior.

The key to effective parenting is connection
The more connected children feel to their parents, the more cooperative, happy, and secure they will be. The quality of the parent/child relationship has a huge impact on children's emotional and cognitive development. Parents can establish a loving connection by touching and holding children, listening to them, responding patiently, and playing with them.

Summary of major points

- Children have many legitimate needs.

- Children have intense feelings.

- Children can heal from distressing experiences.

- Behavior problems always have a valid cause.

- Children don't need punishments or rewards.

- The key to effective parenting is connection.

Hope for the future

This approach to parenting may seem difficult and time-consuming. You may feel that you have better things to do than sit with your children until they fall asleep, tolerate a half hour of angry crying, or play doctor with them. Try to remember that the time you spend with your children when they are young is an investment in their future well-being and your long-term relationship with them. By meeting their needs and accepting their emotions, you will give them a solid foundation of self-esteem and provide them with valuable skills for coping with life.

These early years do not last forever. There will come a time when your children will brush their teeth without being reminded, eat without spilling, fall asleep alone, and read to themselves. They will naturally want to spend more time with friends and less time with you. They are dependent on you now in ways that will soon change, and before you know it, they will be grown up. Cherish your moments of connection, and remember to enjoy the playfulness, spontaneity, intensity, imagination, and curiosity of your children.

If you feel guilty after reading this book, because you wish you had acted differently when your children were younger, rest assured that it is never too late to help them heal and to strengthen your relationship with them. Your parenting style will change as you learn and mature as a person. You have always done your best with the information and resources you had at the time. Appreciate yourself as the caring parent you have always been, and be sure to take good care of yourself.

If we can help children flourish, the entire world will become the place we all yearn for. People will be loving and respectful of each other. We will take good care of our beautiful planet and use its resources wisely. Nobody will live in poverty, and war will become a thing of the past because people will know how to solve conflicts in peaceful ways. Our brilliant minds will help us to discover ever more exciting facts about the universe. *We can make all this come true!*

References and Suggestions for Further Reading

The scientific references in this section provide research evidence for the facts presented in this book. I have organized them according to the topics within each chapter. The suggestions for further reading include books of interest to people who wish to pursue these topics in greater depth. I have selected books that contain useful information and that are fairly consistent with the approach described in this book. Please note, however, that some of the advice in these books is not totally compatible with my approach.

Chapter 1: Tears and Tantrums

Research and information about crying

Barr, R.G. (2010). Les pleurs et leur importance pour le développement psychosocial des enfants. *Devenir*, 22, 163–174.

de Weerth, C. & Buitelaar, J.K. (2007). Childbirth complications affect young infants' behavior. *European Child and Adolescent Psychiatry*, 16(6), 379–388.

Frey II, W.H. *et al.* (1981). Effect of stimulus on the chemical composition of human tears. *American Journal of Ophthalmology*, 92, 559–567.

Gracanin, A. *et al.* (2014). Is crying a self-soothing behavior? *Frontiers in Psychology*, 5, 502.

Karle, W. *et al.* (1973). Psychophysiological changes in abreaction therapy. Study 1: Primal Therapy. *Psychotherapy: Theory, Research and Practice*, 10, 117–122.

Quas, J.A. *et al.* (2000). Dissociations between psychobiologic reactivity and emotional expression in children. *Developmental Psychology*, 37(3) 153–175.

Vingerhoets. A. & ByIsma, L. (2007). Crying and Health: Popular and Scientific Conceptions. *Psychological Topics*, 2, 275–296.

Woldenberg, L. *et al.* (1976). Psychophysiological changes in feeling therapy. *Psychological Reports*, 39, 1059–1062.

Therapeutic approaches involving crying

Benoit, D. & Coolbear, J. (1998). Post-traumatic feeding disorders in infancy: Behaviors predicting treatment outcome. *Infant Mental Health Journal*, 19, 409–421.

Emerson, W.R. (1989). Psychotherapy with infants and children. *Pre- and Perinatal Psychology Journal*, 3, 190–217.

Jackson, S.W. (1994). Catharsis and abreaction in the history of psychological healing. *Psychiatric Clinics of North America*, 17(3), 471–491.

Janov, A. (2007). *Primal Healing: Accessing the Incredible Power of Feelings to Improve Your Health.* The Career Press.

Solter, A. (2007). A case study of traumatic stress disorder in a 5-month-old infant following surgery. *Infant Mental Health Journal*, 28(1), 76–96.

Welch, M.G. *et al.* (2006). Outcomes of parent/child embrace therapy among 102 children with behavioral disorders. *Complementary Therapies in Clinical Practice*, 12(1), 3–12.

Trauma, repression, and dissociation

American Academy of Pediatrics (2014). Adverse Childhood Experiences and the Lifelong Consequences of Trauma. https://www.aap.org/en-us/Documents/ttb_aces_consequences.pdf

Mac-Farlane, J.W. *et al.* (1954). A developmental study of the behavior problems of normal children between 21 months and 14 years. *University of California Publications in Child Development* (Vol. 2), Berkeley: University of California Press.

Thomason, M.E. & Marusak, H.A. (2017). Toward understanding the impact of trauma on the early developing human brain. *Neuroscience*, 342, 55–67.

Perry, B.D. (2000). Traumatized children: how childhood trauma influences brain development. *Journal of the California Alliance for the Mentally Ill*, 11(1), 48–51.

Van der Kolk, B. (2003). The neurobiology of childhood trauma and abuse. *Child and Adolescent Psychiatric Clinics of North America*, 12, 293–317.

For further reading

Levine, P.A. & Kline, M. (2008). *Trauma-Proofing Your Kids: A Parent's Guide for Instilling Confidence, Joy and Resilience.* North Atlantic Books.

Solter, A. (1998). *Tears and Tantrums: What to Do When Babies and Children Cry.* Shining Star Press.

Wipfler, P. & Schore, T. (2016). *Listen: Five Simple Tools to Meet Your Everyday Parenting Challenges.* Hand in Hand Parenting.

Chapter 2: Fears and Frights

Traumatic fears
Watson, J.B. & Rayner, R. (1920). Conditioned emotional reactions. *Journal of Experimental Psychology*, 3, 1–14.
Van der Kolk, B. (2003). The neurobiology of childhood trauma and abuse. *Child and Adolescent Psychiatric Clinics of North America*, 12, 293–317.

Typical fears, individual differences, and indications of anxiety
Aron, E. N. (2000). High sensitivity as one source of fearfulness and shyness: Preliminary research and clinical implications. In L. Schmidt & J. Schulkin (Eds.), *Extreme fear, shyness, and social phobia: Origins, biological mechanisms, and clinical outcomes* (pp. 251–272). New York: Oxford University Press.
Buss, K.A. (2011). Which fearful toddlers should we worry about? Context, fear regulation, and anxiety risk. *Developmental Psychology*, 47(3), 804–819.
King, N.J. *et al.* (2004). Specific phobia. In T.L. Moris & J.S. March (Eds.), *Anxiety disorders in children and adolescents* (2nd ed.), 263–270. New York: Guilford Press.
Olino, T.M. *et al.* (2013). Gender differences in young children's temperament traits: comparisons across observational and parent-report methods. *Journal of Personality*, 81(2), 119–129.
Robinson III, E. & Rotter, J. (1991). Children's fears: Toward a preventative model. *School Counselor*, 38(3), 187.

Exposure therapy for fears
Jacob, R.G. & Pelham, W.E. (2005). Behavior Therapy. In B.J. Sadock & V.A. Sadock (Eds.), *Comprehensive Textbook of Psychiatry* (8th ed., pp. 2498–2548). Philadelphia: Lippincott, Williams and Williams.
King, N.J. *et al.* (2005). Childhood fears and phobias: Assessment and treatment. *Child and Adolescent Mental Health*, 10(2), 50–56.
May, A.C. *et al.* (2013). Evidence-based behavioral treatment of a dog phobia with young children: two case examples. *Behavior Modification*, 37(1), 143–160.

Benefits of laughter
Bennett, M.P. & Lengacher, C. (2006). Humor and laughter may influence health: II. Complementary therapies and humor in a clinical population. *Evidence-Based Complementary and Alternative Medicine*, 3(2), 187–190.
Bennett, M.P. & Lengacher, C. (2008). Humor and laughter may influence health: III. Laughter and health outcomes. *Evidence-Based Complementary and Alternative Medicine*, 5(1), 37–40.

Fernandes, S.C. & Arriaga, P. (2010). The effects of clown intervention on worries and emotional responses in children undergoing surgery. *Journal of Health Psychology*, 13(3), 405–415.

Ventis, W.L. (1973). Case history: The use of laughter as an alternative response in systematic desensitization. *Behavior Therapy*, 4, 120–122.

Wilkins, J. & Eisenbraun, A.J. (2009). Humor theories and the physiological benefits of laughter. *Advances in Mind-Body Medicine*, 24(2), 8–12.

Yim, J. (2016). Therapeutic benefits of laughter in mental health: a theoretical review. *The Tohoku Journal of Experimental Medicine*, 239(3), 243–249.

For further reading

Cohen, L.J. (2013). *The Opposite of Worry: The Playful Parenting Approach to Childhood Anxieties and Fears*. Ballantine Books.

Aron, E. (2002). *The Highly Sensitive Child: Helping Our Children Thrive When the World Overwhelms Them*. New York, NY: Broadway Books.

Solter, A. (2013). *Attachment Play: How to Solve Children's Behavior Problems with Play, Laughter, and Connection*. Shining Star Press.

Chapter 3: Living and Learning

How children learn (general)

Bonawitz, E. *et al.* (2011). The double-edged sword of pedagogy: Instruction limits spontaneous exploration and discovery. *Cognition*, 120(3), 322–330.

Brinums, M. *et al.* (2018). Practicing for the future: deliberate practice in early childhood. *Child Development*, 89(6), 2051–2058.

Fosnot, C.T. (Ed.) (1996). *Constructivism: Theory, Perspectives, and Practice*. Teachers College Press.

Gopnik, A. & Tenenbaum, J. (2007). Bayesian networks, Bayesian learning and cognitive development. *Developmental Science*, 10(3), 281–287.

Piaget, J. (2001). *The Psychology of Intelligence*. Routledge.

Shonkoff, J.P. & Phillips, D.A. (Eds.) (2000). *From Neurons to Neighborhoods: The Science of Early Childhood Development*. A report of the National Research Council. Washington, DC: National Academies Press.

Gender socialization

Fagot, B.I. *et al.* (1992). Gender labeling, gender stereotyping, and parenting behaviors. *Developmental Psychology*, 28, 225–230.

Hill, S.E. & Flom, R. (2007). 18- and 24-month-olds' discrimination of gender-consistent and inconsistent activities. *Infant Behavior and Development*, 30(1), 168–173.

Iervolino, A.C. *et al.* (2005). Genetic and environmental influences on sex-typed behavior during the preschool years. *Child Development*, 76(4), 826–840.

Knafo. A. *et al.* (2005). Masculine girls and feminine boys: genetic and environmental contributions to atypical gender development in early childhood. *Journal of Personality and Social Psychology*, 88(2), 400–412.

Leaper, C. (2014). Parents' socialization of gender in children. *Encyclopedia on Early Childhood Development*. http://www.child-encyclopedia .com/sites/default/files/textes-experts/en/2492/parents-socialization -of-gender-in-children.pdf

Mascaro, J.S. *et al.* (2017). Child gender influences paternal behavior, language, and brain function. *Behavioral Neuroscience*, 131(3), 262–273.

Effects of parenting on children's learning and academic success

Borak, Z. *et al.* (2016). Impact of parenting style on children's academic success. *Journal of Social Sciences and Humanities Research*, 2(2), 1–4.

Borkowski, J.G. *et al.* (Eds.) (2002). *Parenting and the Child's World: Influences on Academic, Intellectual, and Social-Emotional Development.* Lawrence Erlbaum Associates, Inc.

Brummelman, E. *et al.* (2017). When parents' praise inflates, children's self-esteem deflates. *Child Development*, 88(6), 1799–1809.

Henderlong, J. & Lepper, M.R. (2002). The effects of praise on children's intrinsic motivation: A review and synthesis. *Psychological Bulletin*, 128(5), 774–795.

Mueller, C.M. & Dweck, C.S. (1998). Praise for intelligence can undermine children's motivation and performance. *Journal of Personality and Social Psychology*, 75(1), 33–52.

Zimmerman, F.J. *et al.* (2009). Teaching by listening: the importance of adult-child conversations to language development. *Pediatrics*, 124(1), 342–349.

Learning to read

Gaab, N. *et al.* (2007). Neural correlates of rapid auditory processing are disrupted in children with developmental dyslexia and ameliorated with training: an fMRI study. *Restorative Neurology and Neuroscience*, 25(3–4), 295–310.

Kam Tse, S. *et al.* (2017). The effects of home reading activities during preschool and Grade 4 on children's reading performance in Chinese and English in Hong Kong. *Australian Journal of Education*, 62(1), 5–23.

Rodriguez, E.T. & Tamis-LeMonda, C.S. (2011). Trajectories of the home learning environment across the first 5 years: associations with children's vocabulary and literacy skills at prekindergarten. *Child Development*, 82(4), 1058–1075.

Sénéchal, M. & LeFevre, J.A. (2002). Parental involvement in the development of children's reading skill: a five-year longitudinal study. *Child Development*, 73(2), 445–460.

Snowling, M.J. (2015). Early identification and interventions for dyslexia: a contemporary view. *Journal of Research in Special Educational Needs*, 13(1), 7–14.

Temple, E. (2002). Brain mechanisms in normal and dyslexic readers. *Current Opinion in Neurobiology.* 12(2), 178–183.

Schools for young children

Bowman, B.T. *et al.* (Eds.) (2001). *Eager to Learn: Educating Our Preschoolers.* National Academies Press.

Copple, C. & Bredekamp, S. (Eds.) (2009). *Developmentally Appropriate Practice in Early Childhood Programs Serving Children from Birth through Age 8 (3rd ed.).* National Association for the Education of Young Children.

Marcon, R.A. (1999). Differential impact of preschool models on development and early learning of inner-city children: a three-cohort study. *Developmental Psychology*, 35(2), 358–375.

Weisberg, D.S. *et al.* (2013). Guided play: where curricular goals meet a playful pedagogy. *Mind, Brain, and Education*, 7(2), 104–112.

Screen-based activities

Calvert, S.L. *et al.* (2017). The American Psychological Association task force assessment of violent video games: Science in the service of public interest. *American Psychologist*, 72(2), 126–143.

Christakis, D.A. *et al.* (2004). Early television exposure and subsequent attentional problems in children. *Pediatrics*, 113(4), 708–713.

Schmidt, M.E. & Vandewater, E.A. (2008). Media and attention, cognition, and school achievement. *Future Child*, 18(1), 63–85.

Takeuchi, H. *et al.* (2016). Impact of videogame play on the brain's microstructural properties: cross-sectional and longitudinal analyses. *Molecular Psychiatry*, 21(12), 1781–1789.

Wright, J.C. *et al.* (2001). The relations of early television viewing to school readiness and vocabulary of children from low-income families: the early window project. *Child Development*, 72(5), 1347–1366.

For further reading

Armstrong, T. (2000). *In Their Own Way: Discovering and Encouraging Your Child's Multiple Intelligences.* Tarcher/Putnam.

Eliot, L. (2010). *Pink Brain, Blue Brain: How Small Differences Grow into Troublesome Gaps—And What We Can Do About it.* Mariner Books.

Holt, J. (2017). *How Children Learn* (50th Anniversary Edition). Da Capo Lifelong Books.

Holt, J. & Farenga, P. (2003). *Teach Your Own: The John Holt Book of Home-schooling*. Da Capo Press.

Chapter 4: Playing and Pretending

The educational benefits of play

Bruner, J.S. (1975). Play is serious business. *Psychology Today*, January, 81–83.

Duncan, R.W. & Tarulli, D. (2003). Play as the leading activity of the preschool period: Insights from Vygotsky, Leont'ev, and Bakhtin. *Early Education and Development*, 14, 271–292.

Elkind, D. (2007). *The Power of Play: Learning What Comes Naturally*. Da Capo Press.

Pellegrini, A.D. & Smith, P.K. (1998). Physical activity play: the nature and function of a neglected aspect of playing. *Child Development*, 69(3), 577–98.

Piaget, J. (1962). *Play, Dreams and Imitation in Childhood*. W.W. Norton & Company.

Taylor, M. (1999). *Imaginary Companions and the Children Who Create Them*. Oxford University Press.

Vygotsky, L. (1966/1977). Play and its role in the mental development of the child. *Soviet Developmental Psychology*, 5, 6–18.

The therapeutic benefits of play

Axline, V. (1981). *Play Therapy: The Groundbreaking Book That Has Become a Vital Tool in the Growth and Development of Children*. Ballantine Books.

Booth, P.B. & Jernberg, A.M. (2010). *Theraplay: Helping Parents and Children Build Better Relationships through Attachment-Based Play*. San Francisco, CA: Josey-Bass.

Draper, K. *et al.* (2009). Preschoolers, parents, and teachers (PPT): a preventive intervention with an at risk population. *International Journal of Group Psychotherapy*, 59(2), 221–242.

Oaklander, V. (1988). *Windows to Our Children: A Gestalt Therapy Approach to Children and Adolescents*. The Gestalt Journal Press.

Oaklander, V. (2007). *Hidden Treasure: A Map to the Child's Inner Self*. Karmac Books.

O'Connor, K.J. *et al.* (2016). *Handbook of Play Therapy* (2nd Edition). John Wiley & Sons.

Reddy, L.A. *et al.* (Eds.).(2005). *Empirically Based Play Interventions for Children*. Washington, DC: American Psychological Association.

Rye, N. (2008). Filial therapy for enhancing relationships in families. *The Journal of Family Health Care*, 18(5), 179–181.

Cooperation and competition

Bay-Hinitz, A.K. & Wilson, G.R. (2005). A cooperative games intervention for aggressive preschool children. In L.A. Reddy *et al.* (Eds.), *Empirically Based Play Interventions for Children* (pp. 169–190). Washington, DC: American Psychological Association.

Choi, J. *et al.* (2011). Relationships among cooperative learning experiences, social interdependence, children's aggression, victimization, and prosocial behaviors. *Journal of Applied Social Psychology*, 41(4), 976–1003.

Decety, J. *et al.* (2004). The neural basis of cooperation and competition: an fMRI investigation. *NeuroImage*, 23, 744–751.

Endedijk, H.M. *et al.* (2015). The role of child characteristics and peer experiences in the development of peer cooperation. *Social Development*, 24 (3), 521–540.

Kohn, A. (1992). *No Contest: The Case Against Competition*. Houghton Mifflin.

Madsen, M.C. (1971). Developmental and cross-cultural differences in the cooperative and competitive behavior of young children. *Journal of Cross-Cultural Psychology*, 2, 365–371.

For further reading

Cohen, L. (2001). *Playful Parenting*. New York, NY: Ballantine Books.

Solter, A. (2013). *Attachment Play: How to Solve Children's Behavior Problems with Play, Laughter, and Connection*. Shining Star Press.

Chapter 5: Conflicts and Challenges

Disadvantages of spanking

Gerschoff, E.T. & Grogan-Kaylor, A. (2016). Spanking and child outcomes: Old controversies and new meta-analyses. *Journal of Family Psychology*, 30(4),453–469.

Miller, A. (1990). *For Your Own Good: Hidden Cruelty in Childrearing and the Roots of Violence*. Farrar, Straus and Giroux.

Straus, M.A. *et al.* (2014). *The Primordial Violence: Spanking Children, Psychological Development, Violence, and Crime*. Routledge.

Straus, M.A. *et al.* (1997). Spanking by parents and subsequent antisocial behavior of children. *Archives of Pediatric & Adolescent Medicine*, 151(8), 761–767.

Turner, H.A. & Muller, P.A. (2004). Long-term effects of child corporal punishment on depressive symptoms in young adults: Potential moderators and mediators. *Journal of Family Issues*, 25(6), 761–782.

Disadvantages of time-out

Australian Association for Infant Mental Health (July 2009): Position Pager 3: Time Out. http://www.aaimhi.org/inewsfiles/Position %20Paper%203.pdf.

Hyman, I. (1990). Child abusers' destructive use of 'time-out', from *Reading, Writing and the Hickory Stick*, pp. 139–140, 12–13. http://www.nospank .net/timeout.htm.

Siegel, D.J. & Bryson, T.P. (2014). 'Time-Outs' Are Hurting Your Child. *Time Magazine Online*, September 23. http://time.com/3404701/ discipline-time-out-is-not-good.

Suchman, N.E. *et al.* (2006). Parenting interventions for drug-dependent mothers and their young children: The case for an attachment-based approach. *Family Relations*, 55, 211–226.

Disadvantages of rewards

Deci, E.L. *et al.* (1999). A meta-analytic review of experiments examining the effects of extrinsic rewards on intrinsic motivation. Psychological Bulletin, 125(6), 627–668.

Kohn, A. (1999). *Punished by Rewards: The Trouble with Gold Stars, Incentive Plans, A's, Praise, and Other Bribes*. Houghton Mifflin Company.

Lepper, M.R. *et al.* (1973). Undermining children's intrinsic interest with extrinsic reward: A test of the over-justification hypothesis. *Journal of Personality and Social Psychology*, 28(1), 129–137.

Ryan, R.M. (2000). When rewards compete with nature: The undermining of intrinsic motivation and self-regulation. In *Intrinsic and Extrinsic Motivation: The Search for Optimal Motivation and Performance* by C. Sansone & J.M. Harackiewicz (Eds.), San Diego, CA: Academic Press, Inc.

For further reading

Faber, E. & Mazlish, E. (2012). *How to Talk so Kids Will Listen and Listen so Kids Will Talk*. Scribner.

Kohn, A. (2005). *Unconditional Parenting: Moving from Rewards and Punishments to Love and Reason*. Atria (Simon & Schuster, Inc.).

Gordon, T. (2000). *Parent Effectiveness Training: The Proven Program for Raising Responsible Children*. Three Rivers Press.

Markham, L. (2013). *Peaceful Parent, Happy Kids: How to Stop Yelling and Start Connecting*. Penguin Group.

Rosenberg, M. (2005). *Raising Children Compassionately: Parenting the Nonviolent Communication Way*. PuddleDancer Press.

Solter, A. (2013): *Attachment Play: How to Solve Children's Behavior Problems with Play, Laughter, and Connection*. Shining Star Press.

Chapter 6: Friends and Foes

Birth of a sibling and sibling rivalry

Bennett, J.C. (1990). Nonintervention into siblings' fighting as a catalyst for learned helplessness. *Psychological Reports*, 66(1), 139–145.

Smith, J. & Ross, H. (2007). Training parents to mediate sibling disputes affects children's negotiation and conflict understanding. *Child Development*, 78(3), 790–805.

Simkin, P. (1993). When should a child attend a sibling's birth? A guideline for parents. *Midwifery Today and Childbirth Education*, 28(37).

Tippett, N. & Wolke, D. (2015). Aggression between siblings: associations with the home environment and peer bullying. *Aggressive Behavior*, 41(1), 14–24.

Volling, B.L. (2012). Family transitions following the birth of a sibling: an empirical review of changes in the firstborn's adjustment. *Psychological Bulletin*, 138(3), 497–528.

Sexual abuse

Briere, J.N. & Elliott, D.M. (1994). Immediate and long-term impacts of child sexual abuse. *The Future of Children*, Vol 4(2), 54–69.

Coles, J. *et al.* (2015). Childhood sexual abuse and its association with adult physical and mental health: results from a national cohort of young Australian women. *Journal of Interpersonal Violence*, 39(11), 1929–1944.

Co-parenting after divorce

Lamela, D. & Figueiredo, B. (2016). Coparenting after marital dissolution and children's mental health: a systematic review. *Jornal de Pediatria*, 92(4), 331–342.

For further reading

Faber, A., & Mazlish, E. (2012). *Siblings Without Rivalry: How to Help Your Children Live Together so You Can Live Too*. W.W. Norton & Company, Inc.

Markham, L. (2015). *Peaceful Parent, Happy Siblings: How to Stop the Fighting and Raise Friends for Life*. Penguin Group.

Samalin, N. (1996). *Loving Each One Best: A Caring and Practical Approach to Raising Siblings*. Bantam Books.

Chapter 7: Eating and Ailments

Eating behavior

Allirot, X. *et al.* (2018). Shopping for food with children: a strategy for directing their choices toward novel foods containing vegetables. *Appetite*, 120, 287–296.

Benton, D. (2004). Role of parents in the determination of the food preferences of children and the development of obesity. *International Journal of Obesity and Related Metabolic Disorders*, 28(7), 858–869.

Birch, L.L. *et al.* (1991). The variability of young children's energy intake. *New England Journal of Medicine*, 324 (4), 232–235.

Fisher, J.O. & Birch, L.L. (1999). Restricting access to palatable foods affects children's behavioral response, food selection, and intake. *American Journal of Clinical Nutrition*, 69(6), 1264–1272.

Fries, L.R. *et al.* (2017). Parent-child mealtime interactions associated with toddlers' refusals of novel and familiar foods. *Physiology and Behavior*, 176, 93–100.

Johnson, S.L. & Birch, L.L. (1994). Parents' and children's adiposity and eating style. *Pediatrics*, 94(5), 653–661.

Johnson, S.L. (2000). Improving preschoolers' self-regulation of energy intake. *Pediatrics*, 106(6), 1429–1435.

Attention Deficit Hyperactivity Disorder (ADHD)

Brown, N.M. *et al.* (2017). Associations between adverse childhood experiences and ADHD diagnosis and severity. *Academic Pediatrics*, 17(4), 349–355.

Fuller-Thomson, E. & Lewis, D.A. (2015). The relationship between early adversities and attention-deficit/hyperactivity disorder. *Child Abuse & Neglect*, 47, 94–101.

Perry, B.D. (2000). Traumatized children: How childhood trauma influences brain development. *The Journal of the California Alliance for the Mentally Ill*, 11(1), 48–51.

Van der Kolk, B. (2003). The neurobiology of childhood trauma and abuse. *Child and Adolescent Psychiatric Clinics of North America*, 12, 293–317.

Webb, E. (2013). Poverty, maltreatment and attention deficit hyperactivity disorder. *Archives of Disease in Childhood*, 98(6), 397–400.

Children and hospitals

Bergmann, T. (1965). *Children in the Hospital*. New York: International University Press.

Fernandes, S.C. & Arriaga, P. (2010). The effects of clown intervention on worries and emotional responses in children undergoing surgery. *Journal of Health Psychology*, 13(3), 405–415.

Johnson, M.R. & Kreimer, J.L. (2005). Guided fantasy play for chronically ill children: a critical review. In I.A. Reddy, T.M. Files-Hall, & C.E. Schaefer (Eds.), *Empirically Based Play Interventions for Children* (pp. 105–122). Washington, DC: American Psychological Association.

Lerwick, J.L. (2016). Minimizing pediatric healthcare-induced anxiety and trauma. *World Journal of Clinical Pediatrics*, 5(2), 143–150.

Strean, W.B. (2009). Laughter prescription. *Canadian Family Physician*, 55, 965–967.

Wolfer, J.E. & Visintainer, M. (1975). Pediatric surgical patients' and parents' stress responses and adjustments as a function of a psychological preparation and stress point nursing scale. *Nursing Research*, 24, 244–255.

For further reading

Armstrong, T. (2017). *The Myth of the ADHD Child: 101 Ways to Improve Your Child's Behavior and Attention Span Without Drugs, Labels, or Coercion.* Tarcher Perigree.

Breggin, P.R. (2001). *Talking Back to Ritalin: What Doctors Aren't Telling You about Stimulants and ADHD (revised edition).* Da Capo Press.

Hirschmann, J.R. & Zaphiropoulos, L. (2012). *Kids, Carrots, and Candy: A Practical, Positive Approach to Raising Children Free of Food and Weight Problems.* OO Publishing.

About the Author

Aletha Solter, Ph.D., is a Swiss/American developmental psychologist, workshop leader, and consultant. She studied with Dr. Jean Piaget at the University of Geneva, Switzerland, where she earned a Master's Degree in human biology. She holds a Ph.D. in psychology from the University of California, Santa Barbara. She is the author of five parenting books, which have been translated into many languages.

Dr. Solter has led workshops in many countries and is recognized internationally as an expert on attachment, trauma, and non-punitive discipline. She founded the Aware Parenting Institute in 1990 to help promote the approach described in her books. There is a growing list of certified Aware Parenting instructors in many countries who are helping to spread this information around the world. Please visit the Aware Parenting Institute website for a list of instructors, information about her books, and dozens of articles.

If you would like to schedule a consultation or organize a workshop, please contact her at the address below.

The Aware Parenting Institute
Post Office Box 206
Goleta, CA 93116
U.S.A.

Phone and Fax: (805) 968–1868
Email: solter@awareparenting.com
Website: www.awareparenting.com

What Is Aware Parenting?

AWARE PARENTING is a philosophy of child rearing that is based on research in child development. It questions most traditional assumptions about children and proposes a new approach that can significantly improve relationships within a family. Parents who follow this approach raise children who are cooperative, compassionate, competent, nonviolent, and drug free. The philosophy is described in Dr. Aletha Solter's books.

Please see the Aware Parenting Institute website for more information (www.awareparenting.com).

Aware Parenting consists of the following three elements:

Attachment-style parenting
- Natural childbirth and early bonding
- Plenty of physical contact
- Prolonged breast-feeding
- Prompt responsiveness to crying
- Sensitive attunement

Non-punitive discipline
- No punishments of any kind (including spanking, time-out, and artificial consequences)
- No rewards or bribes
- A search for underlying needs and feelings
- Anger management for parents
- Peaceful conflict resolution (family meetings, mediation, etc.)

Healing from stress and trauma
- Recognition of stress and trauma as primary causes of behavioral and emotional problems
- Emphasis on prevention of stress and trauma
- Recognition of the healing effects of play, laughter, and crying in the context of a loving parent–child relationship
- Respectful, empathic listening and acceptance of children's emotions

CPSIA information can be obtained
at www.ICGtesting.com
Printed in the USA
BVHW041048070219
539717BV00017B/731/P